# POETRY NOW

# EAST ANGLIA 1996

Edited by Kerrie Pateman

First published in Great Britain in 1995 by
*POETRY NOW*
1-2 Wainman Road, Woodston,
Peterborough, PE2 7BU

All Rights Reserved

*Copyright Contributors 1995*

SB ISBN 1 85731 632 0

# FOREWORD

Although we are a nation of poetry writers we are accused of not reading poetry and not buying poetry books: after many years of listening to the incessant gripes of poetry publishers, I can only assume that the books they publish, in general, are books that most people do not want to read.

Poetry should not be obscure, introverted, and as cryptic as a crossword puzzle: it is the poet's duty to reach out and embrace the world.

The world owes the poet nothing and we should not be expected to dig and delve into a rambling discourse searching for some inner meaning.

The reason we write poetry (and almost all of us do) is because we want to communicate: an ideal; an idea; or a specific feeling. Poetry is as essential in communication, as a letter; a radio; a telephone, and the main criteria for selecting the poems in this anthology is very simple: they communicate.

Faced with hundreds of poems and a limited amount of space, the task of choosing the final poems was difficult and as editor one tries to be as detached as possible (quite often editors can become a barrier in the writer-reader exchange) acting as go between, making the connection, not censoring because of personal taste.

In this anthology over two hundred and fifty poems are presented to the reader for their enjoyment.

The poetry is written on all levels; the simple and the complex both having their own appeal.

The success of this collection, and all previous *Poetry Now* anthologies, relies on the fact that there are as many individual readers as there are writers, and in the diversity of styles and forms there really is something to please, excite, and hopefully, inspire everyone who reads the book.

# CONTENTS

## MY LITTLE SISTER

My little sister never really held me,
Only in her heart.
Times we had, good, bad, happy and sad,
Treasured memories I have.
Now she holds someone precious in her arms,
Someone made from her, someone small.
A baby girl!
My little sister, little no more,
Treasured memories I have.

*Jacqueline Smith*


## STEPS TO NOWHERE

A step in the right direction,
Two steps back,
Three steps forward,
Neither here, nor there,

Left or right,
Backwards and forwards,
Turning round and round,
Neither this way, or that,

Up and down,
Back and forth,
Swinging, to and fro,
Sliding from side to side,
Which way to go,

No matter, what way I go,
What direction, I take,
I always end up,
In the very same place.

*Diane Godbold*

## DOCK OF THE BAY

Sitting on the dock of the bay,
Watching the tides roll away.
They've long gone,
Those times of trading.
Into the past quickly fading.
The characters that walked this place,
With rolling gait and salty face.
The inns and taverns they frequented,
Full of local talent heaven-scented.
What stories could be told I know
By those seadogs from long ago?
The foreign ports where they dropped anchor,
For the sake of some merchant's banker.
The billowing sails; the storms; that docker!
The contents of a certain locker.
What would they say if they saw Lynn now,
From their busy vessels' noble prow?
Would they stay to reminisce,
Or would they give this port a miss?
I think I know what they would do!
So, ahoy there lads! Can I come too?
Can I sail away with you?
Can I come and join your crew?

*Philip Everritt*


## THE WONDER

Lying soft across my skin
Such luxury to watch you sleeping
Tenderly tucked into the contours of me

Dreaming light upon my shoulder
Tresses strewn darkly upon my breast
Sweetly sleeping the oblivion of the loved

Breathing easy in my arms
No fear has this simple slumber
Only abandon as yourself you entrust

Seeing night upon your face
Feeling the weight of your defencelessness
Weaving my fingers childlike through your hair

I dare to sleep

*Jennifer Steele*


## POETRY NOW

What is that strange blue light below the horizon?
It shimmers in the distance like a firefly,
Winding tortuously towards me over the darkened landscape
- Contrasting with the pale light of dawn behind it,
Inexorably it seems to crawl along some lonely road,
Still faint, growing brighter as it approaches.
Electric blue. What can it be? An omen?
I'm not afraid, but cautious and wary of it.
I cannot always see it clearly.
Now and then the path it traverses obscures it
Behind mounds and woods - yet
The blue aura above it is always visible,
And indicates its progress.
At times it emerges briefly, dazzling - then gone again!
Excitement fills me as it turns into the straight
Towards me, where I stand - at last. What should I do?
I hide beside the road and watch as,
Now gently opalescent blue, it passes close, so close
- A lovely, smiling woman's face with tousled locks.
She looks ahead - for someone?
But why the head, alone?

*John Price*

## FLOWERS

On Saturday,
I buy a bunch of flowers.
Anemones. Mauve, red, and pink.
Their stamen
standing proud.
Like the smile
on my face,
as I pay the florist,
watching, as she wraps the stems
in pretty paper.

. . . I live in a flat -
with no balcony or garden.
Only flowers
in a jam jar,
upon the table.
Their jewel-bright colours
fire-warm, in the coolness
of the room.

As Friday arrives,
the flowers are limp, forlorn.
I place them in the dustbin,
leaving the table bare.

On Saturday, again,
I buy a bunch of flowers.
Freesias. Yellow, lilac, and white . . .

*Jan Spicer*

## BLACKWATER

Dark night, black horizon,
Lift pray, your gloom.
Make way for silver shadows,
Bestowed by the moon.
Gaze upon the rippling waters,
Dancing silver light.
Like diamonds set in stygian jet,
The glistening waters bright.

Blackwater, friend, lie still, be calm
And soothe the threatening sky.
Dance with the wind and softly sing,
A seaman's lullaby.
Gently, rock the floating cradles,
Save wrecks, in gale or storm
And listen, to the gull's shrill scream,
Unfolding is the morn!

*Valerie Margaret Eve*


## THE NIGHT

Softly he creeps across the sky
With velvet shoes upon his feet
Shadows deepen as he passes by
With open arms the mood to greet.

The weary soul can seek his peace
In the darkest hours of night
When, equalled both, are man and beast
In losing of their precious sight.

Night go silently upon your way
Bring quietness to all you meet
Before the turmoils of the day;
Black velvet shoes upon your feet.

*D A Law*

## HOLIDAYS

The chance to forget!
Down a quiet country lane
lies the perfect cottage.
Our wait has not been in vain,
At last our holiday has arrived.
Now we can relax and dream a little
Outside are plenty of birds on the wing.
House martins nesting under the eaves,
Frequently searching for insects to feed
their young.
Late at night I look for a barn owl,
All I can see are some glow worms,
The barn owl eludes me.
Other birdlife is viewed in our travels of
East Anglia.
At Minsmere curlews, marsh harrier and a
hare.
And though we stay late in the evening no
otters appear.

*Jess Davey*


## THE GARDEN

I stand in the garden, the sun beating down
I watch children playing, they run round and round
But who wants to know me, as I stand alone
In this part of the garden that I have to call home.

I stand in the garden, the cool breezes blow
There's just a few people who come, and then go
'Cos it is a bit chilly, too chilly to bear
But where can I go - I have to stay here.

I stand in the garden, it's winter at last
The snow falls so thickly, the flakes they stick fast
I'm cold and I'm freezing, I can't move my arm
I think that this weather is doing me harm.

But no, I am told, you'll get used to it, see,
Because that is what happens to a thing called a *tree!*

*Mary D Jones*


## OUR PETS

We have not one, but two dogs, Prince and Urma are their names
Since they have lived at our house, it's been all fun and games
They lay in wait each morning, ears pricked and eyes appealing
Waiting for the biscuit bones the pantry door's concealing.
One day I left the door ajar, to answer the postman's knocks
I then returned to find, Prince had his nose trapped in the box
I took the box from Prince and said 'you naughty boy to dare'
And Urma looked as if to say 'he's had more than his share!'
Because they are both elderly, they sleep a lot each day
But about 5.30 each night they jump around and play
Should we just ignore them, they sit there looking sad . . .
Wearing an expression that says 'won't you feed us Dad?'
Once feeding time is over, they trot off to their run,
Tails wagging at the back door, 'please let us in, we've done'
They run across the carpet, making marks with their wet paws,
Flop down beside the sofa and drown the telly with their snores.
There's nothing like the welcome that this loving pair bestow
On our return they're waiting there, with wagging tails, you know
No human being could ever match the loyalty they bring
Our Urma, she's the queen of dogs, our Prince, well, he's the king.

*Heather M Duffield*

# THE UNEXPECTEDNESS OF AUTUMN

One day autumn came unexpectedly.
It crept in amongst the days of summer,
Hiding behind the cooling breezes which
Fanned our hot and flustered faces and brought
Rain to dry earth. It hung about the mists
Of morning and settled in the dewy
Grass, surreptitiously freshening the air.

People went about their lives, unaware
Of autumn's stealth, unaware of the signs
Betraying its approach. They did not hear
The bees lazily humming its coming,
Or see the leaves of trees become golden,
Or taste the tang of the changing weather,
Until, suddenly, it was everywhere.

No-one seemed to know how it had happened,
How it had got from summer to autumn
Without anybody noticing it,
Yet here they were in a different season.
The skies were still blue but not quite the same,
The days had become palpably shorter,
The evenings were full of sombre darkness.

People relaxed into the new season,
They put it on as one might an old coat.
Leaves fell on wet pavements and clogged gutters,
Children yelled with excitement at new schools,
Shadows swallowed up the world; no-one could
Really remember what summer was like.
All that remained was to wait for winter.

*Michael Davies*

# SOUVENIR IN THATCH

A council house has been my home
Since he and I were wed,
But to own my own thatched cottage
Was always in my head.

Like everyone else I dreamed of being
Queen of my own domain,
But here in this little council house
I ever will remain.

My kids, when asking 'what shall I draw?'
Got the usual suggestion from me,
'A house, with a nice thatched roof, dear,'
It was all I ever saw.

Came the time when my youngest daughter,
'A' level art about to take,
Asked the usual heartrending question,
'Mum, what shall I make?'

'Make a house dear,' I said without thinking,
'One with a nice thatched roof,'
'That's all you ever think of!'
She chided me with reproof.

Now all three of those kids of mine
In their own property are dwelling,
And still I don't own this council house,
Which the corporation is selling.

But on my sitting room mantelpiece,
My own thatched cottage stands,
A sentimental souvenir,
Made by a loving child's fair hands.

*Mary Aves*

## WINTER

A twist, a curl
A smile unfurled,
In reply:
A remorseful glance
Upon the ground -
   kicked, bruised and lost amid the rush
   of this maddening crowd.

The Church steeple
   slants bleak against heaven.
Pebble clatters and rolls to heel,
Sharp thwack, blast of breath, draft hissed:
   memory, regret, bear to feel
   the past opportunities missed.

Silhouette of naked trees -
Warped,
Uneased,

Pierce with pain.

Wait.

Spring comes around again.

*Sara Weste*

## A CHRISTMAS MEMORY

Many years ago . . .
Thirty three, in fact.
Here is a Christmas memory
I take from those I've stacked.

Two days before that Christmas
I returned home on the train
To be with . . . my two tiny children,
My Husband. And my Mum again.

Oh! How the family loved
That present I brought home with me
It needed no Christmas wrapping
Neither . . . did it hang upon the tree.

It had head and tail, and four long legs
With the children she loved to run . . .
Buster! An Alsation, Labrador cross,
Yes . . . My Guide Dog number one!

*Ivy M Wright (Neé Marjoram)*


## LET GO

I tried to keep hold of the butterfly,
Its beauty was too much to lose,
My fingers tightened around it,
It turned into dust on my shoes.
I reached for the last rose of summer,
The season I'd never let pass;
My hands engulfed the rich velvet -
It fluttered in shreds to the grass.
I tried to hang on to my beautiful child,
His world would be all here with me,
I bound him up in invisible chains -
He resented, rebelled, and broke free.
Our most precious things are so fleeting,
How much time we have, we'll never know;
The way we will keep them forever -
Is to hold them, and then let them go.

*Jacqui McKay*

## THE SWEETIE SHOP

Clatter clatter on the stair
(Sandalled  feet in a flurry)
Just one thought, without a care
The Sweetie Shop - let's hurry

With windows tall, matching pair
And centre door as entry
Bell that rings *as in the air*
To bring the serving Lady

So much choice everywhere
Sweets galore and Grocery
Bird seed too among the wares
Childhood thoughts - what memory

Some children stand and stare
Wishing for a half-penny
To spend on goods displayed there
Perhaps - dark treacle toffee

Others with a coin to spare
Indulge goodies most tasty
Sugary things, some now rare
From humbugs to pink candy

Cashews and liquorice fare
Favoured by Stan and Eddie
As bag clutched in hand declare
Run, laugh and skip - so merry

All have grown, who used that stair
(Sandalled feet in a flurry)
Reflecting past with a prayer
The Sweetie Shop - let's hurry

*Ellen Wayland*

# FREEDOM'S NOISE

Tonight the birds are singing
louder louder it seems than any other night
for tonight I have no threads of thought to sound
Always at this time when the days come to rest
I try to touch all at once but tonight
my ears focus with precision
on freedom's caustic song
Thus no liniment of emotion can seal emotionss wound
I feel the bird's cry can sense the Achilles brain
How can life become the bane of an existence?
Convoluting threads I assure are already quite twisted
In sunshine's embrace I used to think freedom's voice quite sweet
but in shadow's hour
one yearns another kind of liberation

*Joel S Dickens*


# CHRIS IS LEAVING

We have a boss
whom I've never seen cross
By the name of Chris
I think he's rather swish.

He's going to leave us quite soon
I for one will not be over the moon.

A kind and patient man is he
Listens to what you have to say
It will be sad on his leaving day.

We may have it wrong
We may have it right
it's said he could be back
I hope so, with all my might.

*Julie Cory*

13

## NIGHT TIME

The sun sets and loses its fiery glow
Beyond the horizon it sinks so low
To make way for the dusky shroud of night
And a sky softly sprinkled with shimmering starlight.

We look up at the moon from here on the ground
At something so natural but perfectly round
As it casts its shadow down on us all
So near but so far, and deceptively small

At just after midnight it's still shining strong
And continues to do so all the night long
Until it falls with the coming of dawn
When yet another new day is born

But outside my window it's the usual sight
Only the flickering of an old street light
The wind gently rustles the leaves on the trees
They sway to and fro with the force of the breeze

Then all becomes quiet, peaceful and still
The wind fades and dies down as if at will
Then through the dustbins a cat starts to creep
But the rest of the world, it seems, is asleep.

*Rachael Doherty*

## THE GRASS

Before you think this letter's a farce,
I'd draw your attention to the length of the grass,
The front's never been in such a state,
But the back is worse, it's over the gate.

People come to look from miles around,
At the wildlife that is now abound,
And a local lad, whose name is Vince,
Got lost in the grass and not seen since.

Don't bother to visit the local optician,
To see why the people have raised a petition,
For if the grass grows another foot higher,
They think, in it, we'll lose the house buyer.

As the Army refused to cut down the grass,
'The job is too big' said the Top Brass,
'You'll have to get out there and do it yourself,
While you're still young and in reasonable health.'

*Glyn Jones*


## THE ARTIST'S MODEL'S LAMENT

I once was an artist's model
In 1963
But, because I'm so tall
And their canvas so small,
They only managed my knee!
I worked a short time for Picasso
Funny man, used to stand and leer,
Gave me an extra breast, and
Then put the rest,
On my shoulder next to my ear!

*E K Lloyd*

15

## A RUN (IN THE TOWN)

A run in the concrete jungle,
That others call a town,
With one eye on the pavement,
The other on cars that mow you down!

Car emissions,
Double visions,
Cough and splutter!
Fall in the gutter.

A run in the concrete jungle,
Avoiding dogs muck and broken stones,
Ensuring every stride and step,
Will not result in broken bones.

Factory smoke,
Gasp and choke,
Cough and splutter!
Fall in the gutter.

A run in the concrete jungle,
Getting mugged in the underpass,
At least my running should improve,
With so many reasons to run so fast!

Chemical fumes,
Death and gloom,
Cough and splutter!
Fall in the gutter.

*Mark Ringsted*

## GT YARMOUTH

We've the North Sea to enjoy in all its moods
And a beach of fine golden sand
A prom that gives pleasure to both young and old
And two piers that stretch far out from land:
The market place is renowned for its chips -
And many more interesting stalls
The surrounding shopping centre has seats
To rest on, under shady trees, for all.
We've the famous rows that have long stood their ground
Through wars and many crowning of Kings
And the quay with ships that come from afar
To unload their burdon of goods in the crane slings.
We, too, are proud of our ancient buildings -
The merchant house and the old town wall
Our St Nicholas Parish Church is Britain's largest
with Anna Sewell's home close by, so small.
South of the prom is the pleasure beach
With its swirling rides big wheel and dippers
Flashing lights loud music and thrills
Are enjoyed by teenagers parents and nippers:
North of the prom is the water gardens
Adorned in fairylights at night,
A Gondola silently glides under bridges
To pass by trailing willows all dressed in coloured lights
Yes, Gt Yarmouth has much to offer -
Not just in the summer but all year round
And we bloaters are proud of her versatility -
Her grandeur and the history in which she is bound

*Elsa Chaney*

## SEASONS AND REASONS

The year is composed of four different seasons,
for that God does have His very good reasons.
All is part of His balance and plan
for well-being of bird, beast, animal and man.

Spring wakens trees, the hedges and flowers,
lightens our hearts, make happy the hours.
Creatures awake from their long winter sleep,
protected from harm and cold winters deep.

The suns of summer warm body and mind,
giving health and joy to all mankind.
Cold winter forgot in the warmth of the rays,
which bring life to earth through all summer days.

Autumn brings cool and the earth starts its rest,
to recover from giving us all of its best.
As night must ever follow the day,
cool follows heat, this is nature's way.

To rebuild itself to keep serving mankind,
and all life on earth, we must not mind.
But accept each change as part of God's plan,
for all his creation, bird, animal and man.

Then winter comes and the earth freezes fast,
we feel at the time that it everwill last.
But its rest just preserves the life of this plane,
we all live and die, but the earth will remain.

To serve all who follow our footsteps here,
for whom we must always this planet prepare.
So think not of self, but of next generation,
to make safe the world and hapy the nation.

*Madge H Paul*

## JULIAN'S CELL

All down King Street, dressed in gaudy robes of tethered lust,
All down the grubby heaving river they came
Wearing gorgeous badges of wealth and privilege
And the poor, smelling of fish and consolation,
Knights and their steeds, courting life, fearing death,
And Margery Kemp, weeping, anxious, ecstatic.

Still we come, travelling one-eyed, uncertain where we mark our path,
In Heaven or in Hell or both, seeking the cartographer's star
In this still silent place. Maybe it is true what they say,
That all life is mapped out in one solitary cell
And so we come that in this silence wrapped around with clay
Roofed in beams, earth and sunlight met, we might yet hear for ourselves
What we failed to hear six hundred years ago, an answer.

In flinted stone, the unnoted, uncelebrated living pile,
Almost hidden behind twentieth century adorations of style,
Whispers yet of Julian's dream; and sudden faded violet diamonds seem
Cast by the sun on whitewashed walls, to dance the mystics' song and all
Creation pulses there, unsilenced by wars and pilgrimages,
Personal and private, down all the ages. And from somewhere
A stray breath of wind catches at the air and sighs a familiar prayer.

Outside on King Street again, the world does not seem the same
Our steps do not scan the same beat as the roaring road, the dry game
Being played out around us, dreary tat of pimped bondage,
Bags full of consumer goods, indigestible, the trophies of an age;
It is a wonder and yet we know now that all this is behovable
And entirely loveable. It is a wonder that we came here to this cell
And heard what we already knew but would not have otherwise been able
To tell: that all is well and all is well and all manner of thing is well.

*Marcia Parish*

## THE LARK

With my eyes I see Thee,
In all thy beauty around me,
With my ears I hear Thee,
In all nature's sounds that be
Sweetly sounds the rising Lark,
Oh listen well and truly hark,
How he worships in his song,
Rising higher all day long.
Homage pays in his own way,
Wings aflutter the live long day
Heart athrob and pulsing note,
Golden sounds pour from his throat.
Tiny little mite is he,
Yet he strives and longs to see
Heaven's gates open wide,
So that he might there abide,
Close beside thy throne on high
Rippling song to fill the sky,
Precious tiny little bird,
Sweeter sound was never heard.
Happy, happy, little lark.
Plant your song within my heart.

*Dorothy Ventris*


## NIGHT

The wind was whistling in the trees
Much stronger than the autumn breeze,
Suddenly an owl went hooting by
Dancing and singing in the sky.

The air was fresh, crisp and cold
Trees all around stood bent but bold,
A voice in the wind was calling me
To take a walk over, to look, to see.

Not like the day it was very silent
The feeling I got was lonely and violent,
The moon and the stars acting as our light
Shining as a torch in the darkness of the night.

*Kirstie Ann Bines*


## MOTHER - DEAR

There are times when life's sweet apple turns sour,
when your world seems to come to an end.
And it's then that we realise in our darkest hour
on whom we can trust and depend.

You were there for us both in an endearing way,
with an uncanny kind understanding.
A rope we could cling to when clouds turned to grey,
a pillow to soften the landing.

Your guidance and strength is a credit to all,
yet the flame of compassion burns true.
With faith shining forth from an unselfish soul,
and our strength from encouragement grew.

Now the heavens have smiled and sent for their host,
and angel to comfort and nurture.
But let's ne'er forget her that brought us so close,
as we step hand in hand, to the future.

And together we'll share many happier days,
though we pray we can also return,
all the kindness you've shown in your own special ways,
and example for all us to learn.

In you we have found a very dear friend,
a quality matched by no other.
How lucky we are as together we send,
all our blessings to you, our sweet mother.

*Nicola Osborne*

## MY HOME IS THE SEA

Stand on the bridge and watch with me
the raging torrent of the sea.
Whipped by the winds of a vicious squall,
tumultous waves that rise and fall
then crash against the stern.
Oh for the warmth of a home I yearn
but that can never be,
for my home is the sea.

At seventeen I left my home
lured by the call of the sea.
Sadly I watched my mother's tears
but could not understand her fears;
for it was destiny, that I should go to sea.

Before I left I promised to return
and as a Captain they would welcome me.
I knew I had an awful lot to learn
but I would make them very proud of me.

Alas my dream was destined not to be
for both would perish in the cruel sea.
Together they had died whilst in their prime
when just for being Jewish was a crime.
To Palestine they sailed but on the way,
their ship was sunk within the dreaded bay.

Now as I watch my thoughts are far away
for it was fifty years ago today,
we said goodbye not knowing then,
that we would never meet again.
Yet always they are very close to me,
Because we share our home, it is the sea.

*Geoffrey C Payne*

## GROWING PAINS

No photograph survives to show what charm
It was that snared my boyish beating heart.
But promise her I did, that when she came
Again I'd marry her - in red, I think
I said - it was my favourite colour then.
Her parents kindly laughted, and I laughed, too,
To be so well indulged; and so we went
Our ways, I back to childish things, while she
Dismissed my youthful innocence, and sailed -
Her parents, too - the seas to India,
Becoming once again the darling of
The memsahib, her daughter Violet.

The promise was not kept, of course, though meet
Again we did, after several years
Of peace and war had passed. I did not know
What to expect: would she still laugh at me
For childish folly long gone by? Would she,
Indeed, remember it at all? But time
Had dealt a knavish hand: her homeward ship
Was sunk and eighty days in open boat
Had been survived in Atlantic seas.

The teenage puppy fat was gone: the hair, once dark,
Was prematurely flecked with grey; the smile
Now seemed a little forced. We talked of this
And that but not, I fear, of salt - soaked days,
A wound too fresh to be re-opened now.
The eyes now had a clouded look and seemed
Forever scanning distant ocean skies.
We never did recall that promise made
When I was eight - and she quite seventeen.

*C C Waghorn*

## CONFESSION

People speak of love
But there are many ways to love and many ways of love
To distinguish your love for someone is the most daunting decision you'll
                                                    ever make
Other than that of confession.

If you confess your love for someone think not of the sorrow and think not
                                                    of the satisfaction
As to expect anything at all is to expect disappointment
And in the game of love is a passionate and foolish expectation
To confess your heart is to confess your sins of passion;
The beauty that runs and directs your inner soul and being.

Once the confession is done there is no turning of time:
Time will then take you to the events waiting.
But do not confuse time, as time has no real meaning, only desire to fulfil in
                                                    the space provided
Desire in passion and pain
And it is this pain we remember best, for it is this that runs and directs our
hearts resulting in this confession.

*Sophie Pinney*



## SHERINGHAM'S TOWN CLOCK

I stand in the centre of the town,
I can look up and I can look down
At people passing to and fro,
As off to work they daily go.

Many changes have there been,
Since first I came upon the scene;
Sheringham has altered in lots of ways,
- It's not the same as in *the good old days.*

I'm happy when it's carnival time,
They dress me up and I feel fine.
In the centre of action I will be,
The procession always goes past me;

Now Weybourne has its lovely mill,
And Cromer's Pier is standing still!
Holt has its war memorial too,
And Gunton its folly, to name a few,

These landmarks are all my friends you see,
But they don't tell you the time for tea!
So here I'll stand, firm as a rock,
Sheringham's friend, its old town clock.

*J Kaye*


## MESSAGE OF THE BELLS

That lovely old church,
Standing on the hill,
With bells that ring loudly,
Or sometimes are still,

In the sun and the rain,
They seem to say.
The doors open wide,
All are welcome to pray,

For the blushing bride,
Or the mourners in black,
For the young men who went
And never came back.

For the new born baby,
Who just wants a name.
Whatever your reasons
We're so glad you came.

*Betty Coker*

25

## THE OLD LARCH TREE

I remember long ago when I was but a lad
seeing the mighty larch in summer livery clad;
It was so firm and stately and majestically high
and seemed to grow forever upwards to the sky;
And birdsong merged with sounds of breeze
as it played joyfully amongst the trees.

And, there resting childlike beneath the canopy
of green mosaic leaves that were a roof to me;
I would lay serene cooled by its gentle shade
'til evening's setting sun began to slowly fade;
And Western clouds in golden drapes
would clothe the evening shadow shapes.

But, life grows old and thoughts quickly pass
and ideas for tomorrow never seem to last;
And, as the larch in winter sheds its fading leaves
I am left with only boyhood dreams to grieve;
Of sunlit days and happy times
and childish joys that were sublime.

*Michael Moore*


## REFLECTIONS

A marriage partner is like a mirror.
At first the reflection
shiny and appealing
echoes what one wants to see.
Later, time, familiarity
distorts the image,
unless the angle is constantly
adjusted.

*D Russell*

## THE CAT OWNER

I own a cat
I chose him, named him, housed him.
He is mine.
I feed him - answering whined requests for
      waitress-served meals.
I buy his food - humped, heavy ladden with
      supermarket tins.
He waits leisurely, laid-back.
I permit his freedom - the cat flap.
In and out he goes, where his fancy takes him.
I place him on my lap, requesting affection;
He's off, mule-stubborn, through his
      freedom flap.
Yet, he demands the lap of luxury at *his*
      convenience.
Scowls when refused (don't let anyone say
      cats are inscrutable).
He'll fawn when it suites his feline fancy.
My leg, chair leg, - same difference to him
His soulful wheedling whine requests attention.
Slowly, he twists you round his pussy paw.
I am a cat-owned cat owner.

*Nicole Floyd*


## HAND OF FRIENDSHIP

A person who cares,
Whose love is sincere,
Will be a true friend
When trouble lurks near.
As problems expand
And there seems no way out,
Hands offered in love
Prove what friendship's about.

*Madeleine Fitch*

## UNTITLED

I have a lovely garden, for me at least to see,
It's sad there's none to share it, or keep me company,
But at least I have a bird bath,
And how they love the water
They sit around the garden path
Waiting their turn to enter,
I'm not so lonely watching them
They give me so much pleasure,
It seems to me they are an omen
Of a brighter happier future
My garden is the work of one women
My beautiful daughter Pauline,
She planned it, and worked like a demon
With scarcely a break in between,
So my heartfelt thanks my darling,
It's the best gift I've ever had
I don't mind the winter coming
I shall remember this summer, and be glad.

*Iris G Button*


## BRIEF MOMENTS OF BELONGING

She sits there
Hard as any diamond
And just as unaware of her own worth.
Carved in light
Made bright by love
Polished in experience.
I hold her in my eyes
In my thoughts
In my arms
In brief moments of belonging.

*Bill Hockley*

## AN UGLY WORD

It's an ugly word
You can't drop it into conversation;
It's for hushed moments
Of whispered explanations.

It's a deep, dark, cruel
Self-pitying thing;
It's a desolation
Words cannot touch.

It's a tight-lipped silence
When we should talk all night;
It's a dry-eyed numbness
In the eye of the storm.

Good believers have guilt
For every occasion,
But this one is special -
It's a catalogue of *if onlys*
Whispered to a damp pillow,
It's wondering why you're less forgiving
To yourself
Than to any other creature on this earth.

It's a raging fire of anger
That only the passing weeks and months
Can turn to the warmth of memory;
It's being caught out
By unforgivable tears,
It's the thousand slightest things
That were part of a single soul.

It's an ugly word, suicide.

*David Lincoln*

## ABSENT IMAGES

Here in the quiet of this room
I sit alone.
Outside, the wind stirs and shakes the trees
The leaves attempt to stay.
I think of you, I see your face,
Always your face.

The maddening chatter I used to hear
As together we would run
Through the tangle of tall, tormented trees.
Then upon the warm, comforting grass we would lay.
I knew then, life would betray.

You stood motionless
Bathed in the bright, blue light.
I watched you go, I watched you enter,
I call to you, reach for you.
Too far away.
I long for you, want you.
No don't go, stay.

Silence is my companion now,
Tears my deceiver.
They bring you to me, we huddle close
Then weep as the precious image fades.
You turn and smile as you leave me, leave your home.

Here in the quiet of this room
I sit alone.

*B A Fallon*

# EAST ANGLIA'S OWN FARMLAND

In my life this world I have travelled
And seen many a wondrous thing
And heard the different races
Their own countries praises sing
I have climbed Scandinavian mountains
Trod burning desert sand
But nowhere have I seen the like
Of East Anglia's own farmland

Green of every different hue
From the hedgerows, fields and trees
Surrounding flaxen fields of corn
Waving in the summer's breeze
The farmer on his combine
A machine that never tires
He daydreams when he did that job
Walking behind the mighty shires

Those hot lazy summer days
As on the lush green grass I would lay
As skylarks soared and sang with joy
And watch the new-born lambs at play
And when the urge became too strong
For me once more to roam
Thos memories I always carried
Of East Anglia and my home

The folk who hail from East Anglia
Are proud and rightly so
Of their part of this old England
For no matter where you go
No land is more productive
No worker more keen or skilled
An example to the whole wide world
Of how life can be fulfilled.

*Don Woods*

## WOMAN OF WARMTH

Instinet invited, conditioned by life
Holding hope by the hand. A smile
for sisters in sadness, neighbours in need
Their confusion stacked in a pile

Arms outstretched, acceptance home
Sympathy stored in a drawer
Effluent empathy close at hand
For the muddled minds at the door

Hidden by heart, her fervent wish
For the gifts to be returned
From the broken spirits softly soothed
By a warmth unknown yet learnt.

*Maxine D English*


## OUR MGB

Moving down the winding road
Trees arched, to form a tunnel green
With open top, warm summer breeze
Makes mind toward nostalgia lean
Through the Rodings, Leaden, Abbess and white
These leisurely moments we would seize
The thatched cottage at Abbess, it's garden
Where we dwelt awhile, and took cream teas
Then to North Weald, the old air-field
Famed fighter base of World War II
Perhaps a show of fighter planes
Remembering those, we called the few
Move now North through Finchingfield
The old steam trains near Manningtree
I remember well those summer days
Those trips in our old MGB.

*Ron C March*

# A MOTHER'S NIGHTMARE

Motherhood, has stirred memories,
with cruel repression.
Abused and used, it hurts.
Robbed of her childhood, her fretting
heart makes her soul opaque.

It broke her Mother's heart.
But the counsellor, in his wisdom,
thought he knew best.
'Tell your mother,' he suggests, ' and you
will feel better.'

Pulled from her pedestal, she thought
she had got it right.
Her off-spring is her delight.
Now their nightmares begin.

Her child now haunted by days past.
Violated by an evil leech, injured in
her flight for life.
Now wants answers, reassurance
and forgiveness for her penitence.

But always she will be faultless
in her mother's eye
And sinless in God's.
No victor, for evil parasites.
Just immeasurable love to colour the
opaque soul.

*Sheila Price*

## EVACUATION MEMORIES

Waiting children line after line.
Weather outside is not too fine.
I catch confused smiles though most are sad frowns.
Away from this countryside, we miss our home towns.
Little hands full with rucksacks and gas masks.
Soldiers outside are longing for hot flasks.
Faces grubby matched with tired, naive eyes.
Weeping for home in pitiful cries.
I feel so lead heavy my body can't cope.
My thoughts do not matter, my face is my hope
*Too small* or *too tall* excuses amount.
*Too fat* or *too thin* - appearances count.
Then suddenly a finger is pointed at me.
A sharp finger piercing is all I can see
Time to pick up luggage, little sister and teddy bear.
We'll finally eat, there might be a treat! So wash your
                              hands and brush your hair.

Dinner was horrid, pancakes and gravy.
I wish Dad was home, home from the Navy
Hope nothing's happened to him. Hope he's not dead.
Not allowed to worry now, I've been told too go to bed.

Turning in a new bed looking up at a new ceiling.
Praying a bomb won't fall. What a horrid feeling.
Now it's only a little sister and I we must work as a team.
An end to this painful war is only a distant dream.
I'll take us home soon we'll escape all this sorrow.
But first let me rest. I'll deal with that tomorrow.

*Jessie Leigh Klass  (14)*

## WHY?

Why do we hold on to the pain inside?
It would have been better if we'd cried
To let it all out; extinguish the flames
Who's to judge and who's to blame?

I want a new start - I want to be free
I want them to see another me
With dreams in my heart of passion and love
Perhaps it'd be better if I went up above
To find the reason for this strife
For the anger and sorrow in my life

I want to be rid of the pain and the rage
To be as free as a bird - to open the cage
To a peaceful life and a peaceful soul
I want direction, ambition and a worthwhile goal

To hold my head high, to pay my dues
I want to win - not to lose
In life's lottery, the game, the stakes
To wipe away all the mistakes

I want to get things in perspective
Instead of being inward and reflective
To say goodbye to this old world
And see a whole new life unfurled

Why can't I say no to negativity?
And open up the real me
To stand for once on my own two feet
To claim for once my rightful seat

'I am me!' - I shout out loud
Then they'd listen the whole of the crowd
To what I say and who I am
I'll say what I think and won't give a damn

*Michael Fincham*

## PEACE

We long for peace in our time
all over the world, for all mankind,
the suffering of war
not God's law.

Innocent victims, for peace they yearn,
homes and lives destroyed, will we never learn,
we today remember the past
we pray for world peace, peace that lasts.

Is it too much to ask
is it such a hard task,
to show compassion to the weak
to turn the other cheek.

One life is all we have to live
to help each other, to love to give,
for all too soon, end of life span
too late then, for man.

How will we stand on judgement day
when the life God gave, he takes away,
was our life here below all in vain
will we hang our head in shame.

Or will we say with truthful heart
through some small deed we did our part,
and if we always try to do our best
dear Father, grant us peace, and eternal rest.

*Millicent Hewitt*

## TWO'S COMPANY

I think I'll take a trip to the moon,
The old witch said to her cat,
'A trip to the moon? Did you say oh witch,
'That's right - I did say just that.'

'May I come with you dear witch to the moon?
The journey I know I'll enjoy.'
'It depends,' said the witch, 'on how you behave
So make sure that you are a good boy.'

'I'll polish your broomstick and make it like new,
Your cloak I will wash nice and clean,
Together we'll fly to that man in the moon,
Like two space-men, - if you see what I mean.'

'You take too much for granted, you silly old cat,
Why should I take you to the moon?
I can do what I want if I go on my own,
So tomorrow I'll start about noon.'

The next day she set off on her broomstick so bright,
And into the heavens she soared,
But after a-time she returned for the cat,
For she knew he'd be lonely and bored.

The cat's eyes lit up as the old witch returned,
And his mouth widened into a grin;
'I knew you would miss me and have to come back,'
He said - as she tickled his chin.

So early next day, once more they set out
To see that old man in the sky,
And to this very day they have never come back
And no-one can understand why.

*P Raven*

## KINGS CROSS STATION

White cloud passes, reveals the moon,
Two hours and then the dawn, how soon
It comes when one is not alone,
'But I am' is e'er the weary groan.

Twelve hours have passed since people came,
And rushed to get back home again,
But see now what a lonely place
It is, with but one, gloomy face.

This station at the hour of four,
Shelters those who have no more
Comfort, and a bed their own,
No family, no friends, no home.

A ring of laughter shatters the gloom,
All heads turn. 'There is no room
For happiness, on our station here,
Leave us alone! Can't you hear!'

The source of joy appears to all,
A girl and a youth - quite tall
He is beside his friend,
They are *beginning,* we are *end.*

Hand in hand they onward walk,
Silent, but their eyes still talk.
'Tis the language of dreams they fluently speak,
'Tis the language we lost and persistently seek.

'Why aren't they aware of what's in our hearts?'
She whispers, he nods, they agree and depart.
A fleeting glance back, carelessly thrown,
Says 'Poor things, haven't they even a home?'

You're happy now, but beware of tomorrow,
You could be like us, your only friend sorrow!
You, young woman, when you are much older,
Will you look for shelter on that same shoulder?

*Anne Maxwell*


## MY GIRL
*Dedicated to my daughter Vicky*

God blessed me with a daughter,
I thank him from my heart.
Even when we're not together,
We're never far apart.

I thank him for each breath she takes,
The very air she breathes.
And as long as I am living,
I'll tend unto her needs.

Her face so pure and pastel,
Her hair so long and fine.
I am so very thankful,
This lovely child is mine.

Her eyes are like her father's,
For his are hazel too.
And in the years ahead of her,
The boys she's sure to woo!

So thank you God for giving,
This dear child unto me.
For always and forever,
My heart she holds the key.

*Maria Thompson*

## THE SPINSTER

'What's the matter?' I asked of the lady next door,
Her face was so swollen; 'twas painful and sore,
'Oh I've just had a message to say I must go
to the dentist at once, he can pull my tooth now.
But what can I do with my poor little son,
I've to go on my cycle to be there by one?'

The dear little baby looked sweet in his pram,
So I said that I'd mind him; she was in a jam.

I brought the pram round and warmed up his food,
And he sat on my lap; I really felt good.
When *splash,* quick as lightning, he grabbed at his spoon.
The next thing, his food was all over the room.
I stared in dismay while he chuckled with glee,
Then off came the tablecloth all over me.

His little legs kicked and his face went so red,
I managed to clean him and put him in bed.
The rusk I then gave him he seemed to enjoy,
And as he stopped crying, he looked sweet and coy.

Much later, I peeped in, so still he did keep,
I transferred him back to his pram in his sleep.

His mother came back, she really was pleased,
Her baby looked peaceful, her toothache had eased.
'Oh thank you so much' she said looking so glad,
Another time, maybe, I won't feel so bad
About asking for help when I'm in a tight spot,
He'll be toddling soon and around he will trot.'

I wandered indoors and through to the bed,
To clear up the crumbs which were shed round his head,
And drawing the sheets back to air everything,
I saw there a puddle; that capped everything!

*G K High*

## NORWICH CHARM

The city shines and almost glows,
As the Wensum through its city flows.
Flowing on to greet Pulls Ferry
As boat sails past with people merry.
Children shout, and men lay back,
While bikin'ed girls sunbathe on deck;
Imagining some tropic sea,
And wishing things that might never be.
While boats sail by with gentle grace,
The river keeps its soothing pace.
In Norwich City, there's streets to thrill,
Like cobbled road of Old Elm Hill.
Just wander down its cobbled street,
You almost hear those ghostly feet
Echoing from time way back;
Where horse, and cart, made rumbled track.
Those streets are clean, and kept so nice,
For artists it's true paradise.
This city now with brand new Mall,
And Castle on its hill so tall.
The city with Cathedral grand,
Its Norman Tower, how high it stands.
There's many places to give you pleasure
As you wander round enjoying leisure.
You find it's grand as you unwind,
Seeking its treasures you may find.
Encased by ancient crumbled wall.
Its covered market, by City Hall.
This city waits with all its charms,
To welcome all with open arms.

*Eric W T Ogle*

## HOPE IN A CELL

Pilgrims come, lands afar
Seeking salvation, following a star,
Saint Julian's Church, an anchorage within
Its silence speaks to hearts of men;

Here dwelt a lady, fourteenth-century birth,
Destined for fame, upon this earth,
Benedictine nuns her true foundation
A life of religion, eternal dedication;

During an illness, near death alone
A series of shewings, her Lord became known,
Visions of love, *Revelations Divine*
Her spiritually written, gift to mankind;

Words in a window, hope in a cell
All manner of thing, *All Shall Be Well*,
A crucifix of lilies, Christ looking down
Her King of Kings, thorns his crown;

Below a woman, kneels in prayer
An anchoress his chosen, Lady Julian is there.
God is all loving, know him so
Happiness and peace, rejoice as you go.

***Carlyle Allen Randles***

## PEACE

Impressive gates welcome me on
Down a tree-lined walkway
The gravel path opens out onto a green expanse

A wooden bench beckons me to sit awhile
And absorb the tranquillity of this place,
Which nature has claimed as her own

Starlings roost in the winter trees
Like shimmering leaves
Filling the air with their chatter

Clusters of flowers, in various hues, call attention
To the neat rows of black and white stones
As the grass ripples in the breeze

My spirit takes flight with two black crows
Who leave the earth behind
For the pleasure of a cloudless horizon

I feel vibrant and alive, freely enjoying
The colours and sounds which nature creates
In this place - where we bury our dead

**Andrina Manning**


## WINGLESS ANGELS

If we stop breathing, the wind will stop blowing.
If we cease crying, maybe the rain will cease falling.
But if we stop smiling the sun will never shine.
Keep your eyes open and the heavens will shimmer.
Wingless angels keep trying;
Don't rest,
Your time will arrive.
It's a mess,
I know;
But with our eyes closed it becomes the greatest test.
So don't hold your breath,
Show me your hands and light the skies.
Wingless angels hold on tight,
And we will be able.
If you stop living, the wings will stop growing.
If we stop loving?

*Nina Wightman*

## THE GIFT OF LIFE

Is the first glimpse of anew beginning
A Grandaughter in all her innocence
The smile that gives all and asks for nothing
The small hand clinging to our finger
The first tooth, the first word, the first stop
These are the wonders of a new life
She puts her arms around your neck
Looks into your face with a huge smile
Innocence rewarding you with a cuddle
A kiss expressing trust and love
This is the gift of a new life
If only we could shield her from the rigours of life
Emotions of love, hatred, generosity, meanness
Jealousy, loyalty, trust and awareness
These emotions she will experience through her life
Grandparents give love without demands
Watching from the sidelines
Hoping she achieves the goals she sets out to seek
Hoping life will be good to our Grandaughter.

*Barbara Armishaw*


## UNTITLED

March the gentle lamb she takes,
Spring graces April with a crown of calm,
and night for lover's sakes is dark,
and their quick passion warm.

Come soon the night to comfort me around,
With dreams before my sight,
'Ere I wake than days have found,
Into an unforgiving light.

The inky black lays hands upon my brow,
and soothes my restless mood
Which was 'til now,
A winter's interlude.

*John S Howe*


## THERE MUST BE MORE TO LIFE THAN THE A47

Norfolk may not be home: just half of my year
Is spent living here,
So whilst others may write of what it has got,
Instead I shall tell of what it has not.

My friend and I, we borrowed a Nova,
Left UEA behind - no glance over shoulder.
Towards Great Yarmouth that little car mowed
Along what proved to be a long, straight road.

And that stiff road was rather lacking
In any sights with tourist board backing:
Field tree field tree - an eternal damnation,
Would we ever in these lives reach our destination?

my mind went mad with those mumbling miles and was tiring of
tyres that time after time trod stretches of stone as straight
and as level as level allows

We longed for a hill, some kind of incline,
Even a bump in the road would have been just fine,
Something to hide the monotonous fact that
Most of Norfolk is decidedly flat.

What could they do to liven our outings?
I suggest that they build us just one or two mountains,
But when from Norwich to Yarmouth your vehicle is tossed,
At least the Roman-esque A47 ensures that you never get lost.

*Helen Vaux*

## THE ACT

I put on an act to hide my feelings
no-one can get so close to me,
my fear is that one day they will see
my feelings I hide deep down.

I stay by myself so I won't get hurt
my pain is so clear to be seen,
if only I could hide it as if not there
but alas it always shows.

My act always strengthens day by day
the wall grows higher and higher,
no ladder will climb it, no hammer will break it
my thoughts will always be hid.

A lonely life is what I lead
my act is now my life,
the fool I play is just my part
these words are just my script:

*A M Savage*


## ACCEPTANCE

What is this mystical bond between us?
This magical sphere we ride upon.
This tenuous string attached to each other
That carries our thoughts and wishes along.
This unorthodox friendship we came to discover.
The unspoken silence we've come to respect.
The constant awareness of each others' thinking.
The tiniest faults we've learnt to accept.
The crossing of paths in one split second -
that must have run parallel before.
The joy and thanks for what we've been given.
The hope of remaining forever more.

*Rosemary Baird*

## THE MOON PATH

As the moon rises over the trees,
Softly swaying in the breeze,
It makes a path shining bright,
That stretches far into the night.
Which way will it lead for me,
I wonder what's my destiny?
Shall I go along life's way,
With good straight steps that never sway?
Or will I branch off at the least excuse
And finish up with much abuse
From all who cross my path and might
Think that I was born to fight?
Or will it be a path so soft,
That nothing in the way will drop
To mar or cause me any pain
Just like a leafy country lane?
Please may I live my life in full
Exploring down each avenue
And never miss one little chance
To help others as I prance,
Along life's shining path so bright,
Just like my moon path at night.
Perhaps it's best I should not know
Which way my path will go
So as it weaves to and fro
I can *dance* with pointed toe!

*Mary Antcliffe*

## THAT TERMINAL FEELING

From all directions and in every mode
Of transport available but most by road
To the terminal they come to find their flight
All year, all week, all day, all night
The queues form at the check-in the desks
The early morning ones look like wrecks
To the cafeterias, bars and duty free
That's where they go then just you see
In the departure lounge they await the call
To board the plane wife, kids and all
Then comes those words they did not want to hear
'There is a delay,' how long it's not clear
The hours drag by as they wait and wait
For instructions to pass through the departure gate
When at last the call comes they are all very weary
With faces lined and eyes very bleary
But that's all forgotten there's a sparkle in their eyes
As the big metal climbs into the skies
Two weeks in the sun will seem very short
Because you go through it again at the return airport!

*Clive Bloom*


## THE COBWEB

'Come and see, oh come and see,
The crisp white tracery!
Like decorations on the tree
At Christmastide.' November now
Early mist seeps between the trees.

'Come and see, oh come and see
The spider spin her web.'
Catching first one stalk and then another
She cross and re-crosses.

Slowly the web forms.
Until at last she sits
Full centre in her orb
Waiting.

*Patricia Shepperson*

## LIFE AND BEYOND

I was born into this world,
So young and innocent,
Strange people, strange languages,
So many things to learn and discover,
Soon I'd learnt and discovered everything.
Walking through a dark passage,
Turning no corners,
Walls closing in on me,
No light at the other end
Death is taking over.
You're free,
Open space all around,
Everything pure and clean,
It's Heaven,
Forgiven of all your sins,
Reborn into a new life.
A passage with glowing red lights,
Eerie shadows passing by,
Discomfort and hate,
Everything so strange,
Why am I here?
Your sins, your sins,
Hell will not forgive you.

The End . . . or is it?

*Zoe Tabi*

# I WISH

I wish I was a bird
flying in the sky
perhaps a seagull
flying along the shore.

All the things I wish for
not one of them ever comes true
perhaps it's me
I just don't have a clue.

If I could wish however
for just one little thing,
I would wish for people
to except me for just what I am.

*M Gray*


# BANKING DREAMS

Banking dreams for interest
The imagination must be commercially viable
Privatise it
Sell it back to the masses
Open your mind to the voyeurs who have none of their own
Let them feed on worms of doubt and snakes of fear
Sate their hunger
Build their strength
Watch their imaginations grow fat on your ideas
As your own imagination dwindles
Eaten away
Go on feed their dreams
Their vampire lusts
Predators, cannibals, non-vegetarians
Economic growth

*Jennifer Bishop*

## I WISH, CAN YOU?

I wish there was no unhappiness in this wasted world!
Can you see the tears roll down the faces of lonely souls
                                        wishing to be held?
Can you hear the cries of starving people who are praying for   the rain?
Can you smell the reek of death in wars where lives are lost in vain?
Can you touch the hearts of the wealthy with another man's poverty?
Can you teach to a liar the meaning of honesty?
Can you surround yourself with love for all who let you down?
Can you speak for the silenced because their skin is brown?
Can you rescue the birds that are drowning in oil?
Can you forgive your neighbours that have been disloyal?
Can you cure all the diseases that are created by man?
Can you justify to an ethnic the actions of the Klu-Klux Klan?
Can you sacrifice a tusk of ivory before another extinction?
Can you repair the hole in the ozone made by pollution?
Can you swim alongside the dolphins so to avoid the fishing net
Can you offer any comfort to the tramp who's cold and wet?
Can you sing a lullaby to a child who's made orphan in the name of religion?
Sadly the answers to these questions are *No*, all too often?

*Nicola Bell*


## THE JOYS OF SPRINGTIME

Colourful crocuses covering the ground
With clumps of aconites still to be found,
Swaying catkins on the tree;
Giving pleasure to you and me.

Trees laden with blossom catch the eye
With a brilliant background of bright blue sky,
Pale pink petals, others white,
Flowers massed together, oh what a sight!

*M E Bonwell*

## REFLECTIONS ON GROWING OLD

You're getting old, my mirror says - your hair has turned to grey
And is there one more wrinkle there, from just the other day?
The policeman's looking younger now, the doctor's younger too
And I think politicians are less old and far less true

The money now is decimal, the coins are strange to me
And could it be ten shillings they ask for a cup of tea.
The traffic is so heavy now it's noisy day and night
But I recall the country lanes where I rode on my bike

My memory's not what it was, I - who had good recall
And why are things so clear to me of days when I was small?
My life's become a puzzlement, I cannot keep apace
Of famine, drugs and war and strife throughout the human race

I take some consolation that, if there's a heaven above
My friends have gone before me there - those whom I've known and loved
So when I reach the pearly gates to claim my golden band
The ones I've always held most dear will greet me by the hand.

*Charlotte Allum*


## A DAY BY THE SEA

Here we are, we elderly widows,
Down for a day by the sea,
With plastic bags and a Kiss Me hat
And sticks of rock to make us fat.
A jolly lot are we!

It's a chair on the prom and a gin in the pub,
Shall we have a go at the Fortune Teller?
A handsome stranger and money to burn!
Would that it were! But it's only fun.
Oh, a jolly lot are we!

A boat to take us out in the bay,
A cream tea thick with strawberry jam,
Then the journey home and a snore or two,
We love a good time, we really do.
It's a jolly lot are we!

And then it's back to an empty house,
An echoing silence and old photographs,
But just for a day we were young again
And laughed and sang and forgot our pain,
And were a jolly lot!

*Dorothea Gray*


## GOOD NEWS

Have you heard the news today?
No wonder so many feel dismay
Crime and violence are on the increase
and man can't seem to bring about peace
Now for a change would you like to hear some good news?
Why not listen you have nothing to lose
The bible is very encouraging to read
and will provide for your every need.
It tells of a time when no wicked will be found
and of a world where peace and happiness will abound
Where people all will love one another
and treat each man as their very own brother
Now why did your face change as soon as you heard
that these are the promises to be found in God's word?
Instead of listening to what man has to say
Why not investigate for your self today
And then you will see that good news is around
and where it can readily be found
It's in the pages of God's own word
now aren't you happier by what you have just heard?

*C M White*

## OUT OF REACH

And there staring through
her bars, she laid.
And as she looked
reality began to fade.
The patterns of her wall
became fields and forests,
with faces in the trees so tall.
The things she saw charmed
and beckoned her.
But the iron bars wouldn't let her pass.
No matter how much she tried,
Their cold hard reality held her fast.
How she longed to run free
in the sun green fields;
longed to stroll in the forest of wisdom
(would she ever know such freedom?).
She longed to touch the trees
with their hidden faces,
and the ever smiling creatures,
in those out of reach places.
There in the wallpaper beyond
the iron bars of her bedstead,
were all those visions,
that she would carry forever in her head.
So there she laid,
learning all that they could teach,
but with the promise of fun and freedom,
always and forever out of reach.

*Mykael Frances*

## CAMOUFLAGE

Caterpillars on a leaf
Occasionally come to grief,
Worms however can be found
Wriggling safely underground.

A caterpillar chopped in half
Will surely need an epitaph
But if a worm is cut in two,
Two slither off to start anew.

The caterpillar takes a chance
Not worthy of a second glance
Until the day it flutters by
Transformed into a *Butterfly*.

*Pauline Wicks*


## MARTHA - HER AUTUMN

The bare trees shiver, their companion the tangled web of night.
Morning will bring pyramids of red and yellow.
Soon, shimmering crystals will grace the air falling swiftly.
We are privileged you and I, witness to all of nature's change of skin,
and Martha?
Yes, Martha is here, the face in the mirror read, her autumn now familiar.
We are all here, some still in spring, others gazing up to a powdered
eternity holding life's marigold oh so gently in folds of cotton wool.
Amber days riding in on the dapple grey.
Evidence of sweeping brooms left by witchy women.
Martha has known it all, she was here before.
Dressed in black, the wind plays familiar tricks with her hair of jet.
Not wanting to let go she gathers today intimately to her and carries
it into the darkness, together they will face tomorrow.

*Patricia Crone*

## SONS OF NORFOLK

Sons of Norfolk there was no VE day for you, for your
incarceration relentlessly proceeded far across the sea.
For emperor you toiled, starved and beaten, held in contempt
for your surrender under an alien imperial code.
Each sleeper seasoned with your blood.
Each section of track laid on a foundation of Allied bones.
Another day of toil, the air filled crash of the lash - your only pay.
Only you, wives and mothers know the cost of the Burma - Thai railway.

The ripening of the corn,
Hedgerows vibrant with life,
The coursing of the river Yare,
Cuts the county as a knife
would part the fruit of orchards
born of Norfolk soil.
The market days of Norwich
the 'City of the Trees',
The coloured character of locals
and that sweetness of air as the
Cathedral bells peel.

Three years you have yearned for this Norfolk that is home.
To once again return to this place of heart, not breathe your
last of jungle air or last sight of Burmese sky. Of open fields,
gnarled oak trees, the scent of fresh tilled soil, these are for
what you find you pine - once more before you die.
To your suffering no blind eye is turned, your memory fills tears
and widows' hearts bemoan, for you are Sons of Norfolk
- your mother laments your loss.

*David M Pye*

## SOUNDWAVES AT SHERINGHAM

Sounds made by this sea need a pebble soundboard.
Hi-hat waves raking in stone money
Then paying it out again with interest.

An occasional thunderclap as aggressive waves
Thud on their brothers' backs
Or, perhaps, it is distant gunfire.

Sounds of gale blown forest : harsh whooshing,
Branches moaning, leaves foaming.
At its heart, a clearing where a football pitch
Fills with the roar of fans as the last goal wins.

From high up on the beach overlapping waves create
Polite, hesitant concert hall clapping
Which swells to wild applause
Outdoing the performance.

Along the beach soundwaves spread
Like an unwinding coil, sorting the pebbles endlessly.
Soft shooshing breath of Sheringham itself.

*Shirley Jones*


## A LOVERS' QUARREL?

They stood silently,
her head bowed, shoulders heaving, tears streaming.
He tenderly lifted her chin,
seeking to meet her eyes,
while the child sailed leaves and matches
in the roadside stream
unaware of their misery,
they unaware of his game.

*Margaret Francomb*

## THE NEW WORLD

I see the world differently to others
A world that is smothered with covers
Secrets and societies hidden from view
That can only be seen by a few
A conspiracy to control our lives
Of how we think and how we can comply
Big business and governments are the conspirators
They say we are free but to do what
Freedom to travel of which we can not
if we travel by car we can be stopped
For no reason other than suspicion
It is said we have the freedom of speech
But our voices are often out of reach
Every day we work for pay
But are really like slaves in chains
At work at home and in the street
We all get treated like pieces of meat
It is said we control our own destiny
But it does not seem like that to me
There's always someone hanging around
Ready to kick you when you are down
And out in the street with nothing to eat.

*David Allen*


## LOVE POEM 44

Love is not
a makeshift but a principle.

Where the fruit
falls the next tree
will also grow
apples. No oak
nor elm, no beech
nor birch, only birth
and the flesh.

For a naked snake to make
shift without
a courtly coiled skin
in the act of
offering must needs offend
the munching beholder.

The apple tastes good,
never mind the core.
And the pips? Well,
there's the principle.

*Hansjörg Bittner*


## THE MOON STILL SHINES

The sun still rises over Fuji Yama.
The moon still shines on Singapore Bay.
We walked hand in hand in Tangjong Pagar
I remember the moonlight on your lovely young face
But that was long, long ago and you are gone.
I know not where.
They came streaming down The Causeway
They took me to work on a railway bridge.
They took you away from me.
But I know not where.
Tonight I walk once more in the moonlight in Tangjong Pagar
But I am alone.
An old man with nothing but dreams.
How I wish you were here to hold my hand.
For the sun still rises over Fuji Yama
And the moon still shines on Singapore Bay.
But you are gone and I know not where.

*Robert Rockall-Brown*

## UNTITLED

Who is the one who stands so tall
Above the slander and ridicule,
Ignorant of his perpetrator's wrath
Condemning him for lack of tact.
For when it really comes to pass
Judgement day, will come too fast
To reap the souls of sin.

*And the fires burn.*

**S K Zdanczuk**


## TOUCH

Touch means so much
Love grows . . . Heaven knows
Feelings reeling and it shows
Fooling with my heart
I will play my part
Love ever so soft
While it was mine
Heart soaring aloft
When I was thine
For only a day
Now gone away
Was it real
Did I feel
It was not mine
Just dreams in the wine
Love tries . . . Love dies
How deeply I weep
For love I cannot keep.

**Tammi James Weston**

## NORFOLK

Breaking dawn, gleaming like nacre,
Turns to pink, carmine and ochre,
The fleeting colour comes and goes,
Suffused with setting sun, it glows,
As the all enveloping sky,
Far above, arches wide and high.
Stampeding clouds, windmill turning
In servitude to breeze blowing
Way out to the east coast, it goes
Where water of the North Sea flows,
And scavenging seagulls fly high
Swooping with harsh and plaintive cry.

*Lilian Owen*


## VOICES FOR PEACE

Tomorrow's children cannot plead
nor the long-suffering earth protest
against today's destroyers;
nor can our forbears cry,
whose sacrifice and toil,
whose vision and whose faith
helped to create the fragile good
that we today enjoy.
We could so easily destroy this fragile good
by ignorance, or fear, or accident.
For those of ages past are also voiceless.
Only through those who see and care today
the past, the future, and the earth itself
can find a voice,
can plead for peace and life.
Dare we give them a voice to use?
Dare we refuse?

*Basil Bridge*

## SEEKING RAINBOWS

We call it our world - but it's only on loan
For our offspring and the generations to come.
Will we protect and preserve it or destroy to the bone
This planet of ours, this country called home?
The snow covered mountains are now mountains of death
And hillsides of pink heather are burned and bereft
Where once a blue sky, now clouds of grey plumes
From exhaust pipes and chimneys ever spilling out fumes

Rivers and streams, lakes, lochs, oceans, seas
Once teeming with fish but now killed with such ease
We've caught all the cod, killed the seals, whales and gulls
What's left is polluted with crude oil from ships' hulls
Beaches once golden have quickly turned black
Don't destroy this world, it's not too late to turn back
Forests of pine, woods of oak, birch and ash
Are being devastated in mankind's bid for cash
Wild flowers with aroma that pervaded the breeze
Now fill the nostrils with the stench of war and disease

Oh to lie in the meadow and hear the grass sing
Catch a glimpse of a sunbeam on a butterfly's wing
Such dreams are erased in the blink of an eye
Will we stand by and watch with a shrug and a sigh
Whilst the fields are engulfed by battery hens
And the stables a hell for cattle in pens?
No more foxes in meadows, no pastures to roam
Motorways have buried the place they called home
Fields of corn laced with poppies a reminder of war
And of blood spattered trenches, a scene of beauty no more

Yet the sun still shines bright, stars and moon light the night
After storms sometimes rainbows appear
So before it's too late, let's all hold out a hand
To prove that we care for the sea and the land
Our world is entrusted, as guardians we must cherish
Lest all of God's creatures should wither and perish
Shed not a tear for love knows no fear
Only hatred and pollution destroy
The past it has gone and the future's not clear
Were those rainbows illusions - will they once more appear?

*Angela Edwards*


## NOCTURNE

The sombre colours of the night
Softly fold themselves around
And my sleepy thoughts are drifting into memories,
Bringing echoes of days that are long past.

They dart as flickering shadows
Into my defenceless mind

My secret world

And I am led, as by a hand,
Through rooms and gardens I have known.
Elusive faces, voices soft and sometimes clear
Are close beside me,
Only to fade as I strive to hold them.

So many faces, so many voices blend and turn,
Reaching upwards and outwards
Through seasons that are over.

I do not know when they have gone -

Sleep gives no warning.

*Kathleen Howard-Gray*

# LADYBIRD

Light fingers probe loose bark
Warming the inert. They scatter
A rattling red
Bedlam!
Gaudiness unseals to gauziness,
Hoists secreted sails from false colours.

Air is cleft by cutlass wings
Till the rose-ship is plundered.
Red sea shifts and swells as robber,
Mealy-mouthed, sates greed and breeds.
Dark humour embitters the beak,
Red and black not worth the wager.

Jolly-jerkined jester who reviles
Beguiles the child, dottily, spottily
Spotless. Sightless white lies
Disarm the Start-Rite assassin. No sting,
No claw nor tooth, yet blood red
Against the greenness of the child.

A fiery sky belies a cooling hand
That prods the lady home.
All as one they bare the air,
Burn the air and turn it madly red.
Adrift on setting sun they are
Flotillas of the light.

*Sarah Turner*

## ANOTHER TIME IN UTOPIA

July commences warm night and endless days,
Why play football now,
Fatigued of energy perspiration falls down your face,
Diligently they train to impress their manager,
Another training session successfully completed.

A conciliatory match played, cold drinks needed,
Summer ending matches concluded against rivals,
Argumentation begins players renounced,
New challenges commence optimistic of accomplishment.

Autumn approaches destiny has favoured us,
Contests are won people rejoice,
Multitude increases Treasurer commemorates the occasion.

Turf needs consideration continual attentiveness,
Winter everlasting matches suspended,
Money is constricted, chilled climate is perpetual.

Embark on a New Year, promotion seems achievable,
The masses proclaim their everlasting support.

Tournaments are surpassed, performance is evaluated,
The horde assess the situation,
Alterations concluded winning achieved.

Conditions advance accomplishment completed,
Clique communicate full of wonder,
Adventures successfully performed,
Developments seem possible.

March opens birds melodise,
Glebe improves players revel,
Entertainment guaranteed the flock exhiliatate.

Ultimate test success is approaching,
Mission proficient the town proclaim,,
Promotion is achieved people rejoice.

*Johnathan Unwin*

## EAST COAST ESTUARY

Across the strand small grey-green rolls of water glide,
Sunlight flashes chase each other round the curve.
Doomed Medusa strewn, abandoned by the tide,
Motionless in death or loss of strength and verve.

Black-headed waders hunched against the north-east breeze
Like clockwork mice glide shorewards, prim and vain,
Peck at battle lines of rocks instead of cheese,
Called *Septaria* by Roman masons in disdain.

Off the peninsular a tree stump leans against the tide
Mollusc encrusted phallic symbol of Hellenes,
In Elizabethan times attached to land with pride.
What views saw people in its shade? What scenes?

Eastward hangs phlegmatic smudge of smoke from oil
Above quayside freighters loading for EC
A distant pile driver bangs all day in toil,
As ebb leaves cans and feathers, and paper cups for tea.

Sea sage delights the artist and retains sand to flourish.
Sea asparagus, prolific, with healthy, fleshy stalks,
Rooted below high water to firm mud banks to nourish
Those who choose to gather it en route for river walks.

Up river, where hard boulders larger than a torso
Bear saucer shapes and rounded holes etched by eternity
Of years of dripping water from above or even more so
Before the ice age exposed them to harsh modernity.

Harwich harbour dresses for formal evening wear.
Sunset - the Danish ferry looms up like thunder.
Local yachtsmen are alerted to take care,
A Bach fugue organ chord splits peace asunder.

Calm, as the surface of the evening ebb embraces,
A distant train into sunset clinks and chatters.
Yet there is breeze enough 'gainst tide to cheer the faces
Of crew who think it's alehouse food and drink that matters.

*Colin Howard*


## WITHIN REASON

The world of today's in a very poor way,
The trials and troubles are legion.
And people will fight for power or might,
and never consider sweet reason.
All over the Earth there's a terrible dearth,
There's a famine or drought or it's freezin'
But it's always the law that nature is raw,
And not too concerned with sweet reason.
Now some like it hot, whatever we've got,
No matter what weather's in season.
But some will complain that their lawn needs the rain,
So water it well with sweet reason.
When the youth of today is *no work and all play*
And in boredom he contemplates lesion,
If only he would turn his efforts to good,
And temper it all with sweet reason.
When the Government claims it has wonderful aims,
And the populace needs some appeasin'
Instead of a roar from the Parliament floor,
Could they not treat the whole with sweet reason?
I continue to hope as with living I cope,
That my prayers to Heaven are pleasin'
And I hope in my heart when it's time to depart,
That God will treat me with sweet reason.

*Margaret Thorpe*

## A PERSON'S PURPOSE

What is a person's purpose here, I've often pondered this?
I understand a coat, or bike - they're point is hard to miss.
They're useful to Earth's human kind - of this I'm doubly sure,
But when it comes to people, well, just what's a person for?

I asked a man who wore a frock - he didn't seem to know.
He said that all would be revealed when it was time to go.
But when I doubted God could say, he showed me to the door.
He left me wond'ring all the same just what a person's for.

I met a man who mended bones and seemed to care so much;
Who gave his time to saving lives and had that human touch.
He had no doubt about the worth of patients that he saw,
And felt no need to question what he helped each person for.

A woman who had saved a child from drowning in the sea
Was quoted to have later said: 'That child might have been me.'
'Treat others as they should treat you' is universal law,
But even this does not explain what any person's for.

I found someone who loved their life, and lived it to their best,
And put to them my question which, they seemed to find a test.
In answer they would only say, although I begged for more:
'If any person has a dream, that's what that person's for.'

*John Allsop*


## IN TRUTH

Even in fiction there is implanted Truth
As even in life there is implanted death
To some
Death is the end
And life after death a fiction

But In Truth
Death is Transition
And the continuation of life everlasting
But only the end
Of the physical body's restriction

**Rodney George Priest**


## BEYOND THE MOON

I will never ever see
The one who guided me,
Through all my childhood ups and downs,
Her love for me knew no bounds.

I knew that she was always there,
Always truthful, always fair.
Helping me with my life,
Through the pain and the strife.

Thinking of the good times we shared,
She was my friend, she really cared.
Her lovely laugh, her tender smile,
To see that again, I'd walk a mile.

You were taken from me far too soon,
Now you're in a place beyond the moon.
Enjoy the peace, enjoy the rest,
For you are to me the very best.

This lady means everything to me,
A long time together was not meant to be.
Thanks for the great times, thanks for the fun,
Thanks and all my love to you.

My very special *Mum*.

**Elaine Ludkins**

## UNTITLED

Have you ever wished,
   for the day to swallow you up,
To have everything that seems to be,
   be what is not,
And everything your sad heart imagines,
   to be proved a fantasy,
And to dismiss the hurt you feel,
   in guessing games,
That seem so real but hold no reason,
   to be left,
With nothing but the truth,
   but not left cold.

***Tania Freeman***


## STRANGER

You came in autumn,
With gold and ochre leaves,
Chestnuts, conkers burnt orange trees.

I never knew your name,
Never knew your past,
Like the mist of the morning you arrived fast.

Like spangled webs intricately detailed,
Your life may have been,
Dark as night your eyes no-one has seen,

Alert and anxious waiting for your cue
After the mists of autumn we will
Say goodbye to you.

***J Whitchurch***

## STROLLING, WALKING, SITTING

I was strolling through a field,
With corn around my knees,
When I saw a little hill,
Some way behind the trees.
Caught a glimpse of auburn hair,
All tied up in a knot,
Looked like there was something there,
Was it her and if not, what?

I was walking down a road,
An avenue or street,
All I know is there was so
much litter round my feet.
Then I saw a paper, torn,
A scrawl, *love you a lot*,
The signature was faded, worn.
Was it her and if not, what?

I was sitting in my room,
Some crumbs were on the floor,
Just as I picked up the broom,
A knock came at the door,
She was there, she said her name,
Well, what a shock I got,
But her voice was not the same,
Was it her and if not, what?

Was it her and if not, what
was strange about her face,
Did she climb aboard, or not,
The ship from outer space.

*Steve Crancher*

## THE OTHER WOMAN

This time tomorrow the tears will stop
This time next week I'll try and laugh again
This time next year I'll have forgotten
that gentle look in your eyes as you loved me
This time in five years I may have forgotten
the softness in your voice over the phone
This time in ten years I'll have a
half-remembered picture of your face
This time in twenty years we could both be dead
And then we'll be together;
Why not now while we love each other?

*Joan Ward*


## PARTY LIGHTS

Sitting incognito in the dark
Waiting incommunicado by the phone
All alone
In stark
Contrast
To your heart beating fast
Under the party lights.

Guess my invitation got mislaid
Paid
The price for my reserve
Deserve
To walk a different path
From the bright sparks
Who make you laugh
Under the party lights.

*M G Kelly*

## NORTHEY LAMENT

When evening falls on Northey Isle,
Where goose and gull and snipe beguile -
You step through time and rest awhile -
Reflect on Byrthnoth's fall.

Are mud-banks really what they seem?
You close your eyes on Panta's stream.
Is that a war-cry in your dream,
Or curlew's plaintive call?

And do you see a giant stand
Erect and proud with sword in hand,
Determined to defend the land
For kith and kin and friend?

Are those the sounds of spear on shield,
The taunts of men, too proud to yield
To Viking force upon that field?
Or echoes in the wind?

Is that the eagle, carrion-wise,
That soars in ghoulish enterprise
The half-dome of the Essex skies,
All memory to rescind?

The heroes of the slaughter-place
Left not a sign, nor hint, nor trace.
The bloom of Anglo-Saxon race
Here found its tragic end . . .

*Robert Hallmann*

## THE COLD WAR'S OVER

The East and the West are now allies
To their victims that does not apply
For wars have been fought and lives have been lost
Will we ever know the true cost
The excuses they give are not enough
For it's not them who have it rough
Homes and lives were destroyed in an instant
From the flick of a pen that was so distant
Now shaking hands and smiling faces
Both with bad memories from far away places
All the earth has been touched by these super powers
Whose leaders sit in ivory towers
Ordinary people's lives tinged with pain
Who have no interest in political gain
Just somewhere to live and something to eat
A family to love without being bombed from above
And never again to be forced to fight
For this is everyman's right.

*David Allen*

## PARTNERSHIP

Together
      Sharing and forbearing
      Loving and forgiving
      On our good days.
Apart
      Swearing and despairing
      Parting and loud shouting
      On our bad days.
Alongside
      Doing and relaxing
      Contentment is our maxim
      On many days.

Like two dancers, touching and parting,
Each in our way the music we hear,
Sharing the space in movement so natural
Sometimes quite far, but often so near.
Movement and stillness - together we make
A duo - yet separate parts of a pair,
Harmony, balance, enhancing, entrancing,
Interdependence, a quality rare.

Sometimes we've struggled, but deep in our hearts
We acknowledge our need each one for the other
   That gives us our strength
   And keeps us together.

*Marjorie Haddon*


## ENSLAVEMENT

If I don a red cloak
Put on a cheerful countenance
Dance with you across the fields
Will I entice you?
From your enslavement.
If I take you to a circus
Buy you a balloon
Swim with you across the Channel
Jump with you over the moon
Will I free the bonds
That hold you captive
Or is it too late?
Are you already dancing
The dance of death
The slow mournful dance of
Those not freed.

*Helen Reeves*

## A SENSE OF GUILT

As I sit here on this cold and windy night,
I feel a sense of emptiness,
Not knowing what surrounds me.
For if I could find the hours I need,
All by myself during the day,
Not spoken for or to feel guilty of,
and because of others around
I would delve deep into my inner thoughts,
And send all my worries and fears
As days go by clear up to the sky,
For the air to disintegrate.
And be clean like a daisy, to start afresh,
Oh what a nice thought,
But I have to wait for the right time to come along,
And then perhaps things will go right,
And this guilt I feel will slowly fade away,
And I shall feel different,
Hold my head high and be able to think,
What a wonderful world I am living in today.

*Dorothy Smith*




## ONE MAN'S DREAM

Magical Woodland.
Morning's glistening dew
Wild flowers in abundance
Bumble bees drifting through.
Butterflies with gossamer wings
The coo of turtle doves.
The heady scent of Summer
                Oh what paradise.

A little piece of England
Inspired by one man's dream.
A place of natural beauty
Where wildlife can be seen.

Constable left his paintings
Of East Anglia long ago
Ted left a panoramic view
of ever changing scenes
The nearest thing to heaven
          His beloved Wheatfen.

*Olive Barber*


## THE SIGNAL WOMAN

Her narrow gauged excuses she tannoyed,
announcing their time-table terminated,
complaining publicly of connections broken,
expressing a new arrival, and the line she'd taken.

          She had signalled the point,
          and had thrown the lever,
          she had shunted him out,
          as he hadn't wanted to leave her.

Taking stock on a down-line siding,
steaming in coaled solitude and finding,
his juncture on a rolling decline,
he disembarked from a paralleled sanguine,
For coupled destinations she had put to the axe,
just like those uncoupling Beeching acts.

So with ticket clipped; *Return single*
hearth clinkered, and no embers to rekindle,
no cast iron grip, on the overnight sleeper,
he let the clutch slip, from the tender keeper.

*Paul Banos*

## PULL YOURSELF TOGETHER

Pull yourself together girl,
That's the answer for you.
Stop feeling sorry for yourself,
Haven't you anything better to do.

Those tears you cry are crocodile tears,
And they are not for real.
You're so full of self pity,
What's the matter with you?

Smile, it may never happen,
You've got so much to be thankful for,
There's always someone worse off than you,
Life's for living! That's what it's for!

Now pull your socks up!
Just get your act together!
Put your best foot forward
Whatever the weather.

So I'm going to shake a leg,
And stand so tall,
Look the world in the eye,
And tell them all what they can do!

*L Reading*


## THE BLUE HORIZON

The soft, smoky blue of linseed,
Opening its eyes in the sun,
As if only blue skies are worth reflecting.

Or vast acres of earth-bound sun,
With that sharp, sweet, pungent scent.
Icarus's feathers perhaps, or honey burnt.

Golden fur of ripened barley,
Harvested for animal feed
Or to quench our thirst as we watch others play.

The green of wheat so soon becomes
Tawny in the evening light.
Bales made of amber straw turn to trolls at night.

The fallow fields with poppies glow
'Till ploughed deep at year's end
And furrows of clay are left for winter's work.

Only beet has no special charm.
No infant eyes appealing,
To turn our fields to a blue horizon.

*Gail Harland*


## ARACHNOPHOBIA

Have you ever considered,
The case of the spider,
With miles of silk,
Wrapped tight up inside her.

Why this poor creature,
Gets so much bad press,
Only a genius,
Could spare time to guess.

While happily crawling,
Close by where you're sat,
It creeps near your hand,
And . . . *splat,*
It's flat

*Amber Walden  (13)*

# ISLAND

Out of a blue and shining sea
An island shows itself to me
Mountains, bays, a fertile plain
Windmills, caves - I'm home again.

My second home is resting there
Friendly, tranquil, waiting to share
Secrets of its ancient past
A happy place for me at last.

The sun, the sea, the friendly folk,
The peaceful life - all these evoke
No rush, nor hurry, just lazy days
With sights to see that just amaze.

Fields full of crops in fertile soil
Animals and men - hard at toil
Trees a plenty at every turn
Nature at its best - for these I yearn

Olives, almonds, carobs to gather
Strawberries, potatoes - which would you rather
Towns and villages all worth seeing
On such an island it is well worth being.

The way of life is happy and slow
Much too hot to come and go
A drink, a meal, a sit, a chat
Where else in the world is it just like that?

Monasteries, churches, buildings of class
But always tourists there - en mass
A holiday haven for all kinds of guests
Let's hope its beauty remains at its best.

*A Englert*

## A VERY OLD LADY

'I am in a difficult position' she says.
I know what she means.
She has forgotten who I am and the unfamiliar scenes
Of my home and her condition of extreme old age have disconnected her
again.
She is lost, anxious and alone and the pain
Is in her voice, too proud and polite to ask
For help. I return to the task.
'I am your daughter in law. You are in the house of your son.'
The shadow lifts. Now she knows
Briefly, 'till the next time the woes
Of memory loss descend, the one
Gift is that malice goes too.
She forgets the recent hurt as fast
As the recent joke. The last
Telling might never have been.
And the new laugh is as fresh and enjoyment as keen
As yesterday's.
But has she forgotten him, that gentle man?
In a picture he is always *My husband*, never his name.
This is our sorrow. Though he had some fame
Among his kind. For fifty years
He was her companion through a time of fears,
To peace, contentment, and no small success.
Let her remember him, Lord, we pray
A spark of comfort in another weary day.

*H M Liebeschuetz*

## OPPOSITES ATTRACT

Pages of his mind appear illegible,
Written down in an abstract form,
Creating a language that waxes and wanes,
Like a moon disappearing, emerging far brighter,
But still too distant for my eyes to focus,
As the light blinds my fragile perception,
Enduring the puzzles laid forth for solution,
Finding no match twixt appeal and repulsion,
Laying foundations for this insane attraction,
Defying all Nature, respecting no boundaries,
And ending in purest affection!

*M L Dexter*


## PHRASES THAT SHOULD BE BANNED

'Feel good factor'
'Friendly fire'
'Cheer up it might never happen'
'Safe haven'
'Necessary downturn'
'Say cheese'
'Ethnic cleansing'
'God fearing'
Midterm blues'
'Collateral damage'
'Feverish atmosphere at Westminster'
'Information superhighway'
'I don't love you anymore'

*Robert J Gay*

## NORFOLK BOWL

Bronze sky, then, the heat rare:

For this landscape the potter
Abandoned blues and greens,
Stained half of a shallow bowl
With metallic oxide,
Glazing the rest in gold
And buff and brown so that
Its sands and shore curve out
Devoid of plants or animal,
Being wholly chemistry,
Force seeming inevitable
Nor any chance in beauty:

Yet all judgement's creature,
Naming virtue, forming sky.

*Jane Wight*


## CATCHING UP WITH OLD FRIENDS

'This is a blast'
said the guy from the past
to the girl with the cast

'Why d'ya phone?'
I was home and alone
she replied

Then she cried
real tears
for the years
and the fears
and he said
'Let's stay friends'
then it ends.

*S Lewis*

# STORM AT SEA

When morning came,
The horizon and starkness of the groins,
Were phased out in mist.

The rain, filled the promenade
Ankle deep,
The sand, wet, even before the incoming tide,
And the cove gave away
Its lone tenancy to me.

Old Thunder God, Thor,
Released pent-up anger,
Swept out, surplus crashes from his floor.

The sound
Rebounded from the cliffs,
Echoed further than eye could see,
On and on for evermore!

The sea, my eyes, my face,
Reflected
Lightning, that painted crazed orange flashes,
Through a century of space.

Huddled seagulls,
Stood dejected,
And waited for the storm to end,
One walked stiffly on stilted legs, hesitated
Pecked, then walked towards nothing,
Staring into its thoughts,
Bird-brained! . . .
Only they and I beneath the sky!

And all the hours that morning  had . . .
It rained!

*Molly Wrigley*

## TALKIN' BOB BLUES

Bob said he was goin' east, headin' out today
Did I want to come along, did I want to play?
We were bedroom rock and rollers, I still got him on cassette
I'd sometimes help him with the chords he couldn't get

Bob said he was lookin' for a buddy to go further than we'd been
I looked out the window I could see it turning mean
'Bob, there's snow a comin.' Are you sure the roads are clear?
'I don't mind hitchhikin', but why not stay and have a beer?'

Bob was pretty stubborn, he just shook his head and said
'Today's the day I'm leavin'. Tomorrow I might be dead.'
So I stepped to the doorway, I could feel the ten below
Said 'Well, Bob, if you're goin', I hope it doesn't snow.'

Bobby said 'I'll catch you if you ever take the track.'
The last I saw was his guitar, bangin' on his back
The rest they say is history, I got a steady job
Stacking plywood at the timberyard, clockin' in and out . . .

We all waited to hear from Bob, but he never dropped a line
Funny we all thought he was pretty good at rhymes
I bought myself a bungalow, out of the pulp mill smoke
Go out fishing some days, have the occasional toke

Maybe one day he'll come back to the high school reunion
Or I'll be on a tourist bus, see him busking at Grand Union
Aw that's the breaks I guess, hope he didn't crash
Still with a name like Zimmerman he was never gonna be flash.

*Rick Sheppard*

85

## SUMMER'S AWAKENING

January comes and the winds do
blow
The snow it falls so deep
When one looks across the fields
The world it seems asleep
February is just the same, as the month
before frosty days fresh north winds
At times it shakes your door
As the months go slowly by
We will all see a bright new dawn
One morning when you awake
The month of May is born
This day will bring such wondrous things
Leaves glimmering on the trees
The flowers they slowly lift their heads
tormented by the bees
The birds will sing
The grass grows green
The sun will shine each day
One of life's many pictures
To help us all on our way

*Brian Hill*


## FIFTEENTH OF AUGUST

Pale pink roses with the glow
Of a summer evening sky.
Larkspur spikes, sharp bright blue,
Scented yellow gold freesia,
Reminder of warm sun
On forest picnic days.

White lily petals streaked red
With the spattered blood
Of harsh words uttered
During ice-cold February
Leaving the deep crimson wound
Of a single freesia.

Tears falling, splashing, freezing,
White frilled carnation snowflakes
That melted in the Spring with
Symbiosis of like minds.
Will there be red roses next
In my bouquet of memories?

*Ionne Hammond*


## UNTITLED

I stand alone, lost in time,
Taking my bearings after the climb.
Where is the world I'd glimpsed before
When standing wind-washed on the shore
Down there the incessant beat of waves
The vast expanse of watery graves
The empty homes crushed by our feet
The eroding cliffs where seabirds meet.
I'd absorbed all these deep in my soul
Whilst as Custodian I'd filled my role
At one with God in the evening air
I'd felt so humble breathing there.
But now the family's all around
I'm Mum once more and on different ground
The waves and shore are sea and sand
Where one swims and digs and peace
                    Seems banned.

*Janice Thornton*

## IMAGES OF MIND

If I could draw them I would paint
The pictures in my mind.
I'd paint the skies the deepest blue
White wisps of cloud a scudding through.
The broad-leaf trees I'd paint with vigour
In bright green green and burnt sienna

If I could draw them I would paint
The cornfields in my mind,
For in these fields of golden hue
Ox-eye 'n poppies are peeping through.
And here and there amidst it all,
Sedge-like grasses growing tall.

If I could draw then I would paint
Bridges of all kind,
Smith fashioned iron, its curlicue
Casting shadows o'er the view.
And one I'd paint in snowflake white
Refracting light on a moonlit night

If only I could draw then paint,
These images of mine,
Minutiae of rainbow hue,
Flora, fauna, people too,
I'd give the arts a novel slant.
But I confess - I fear I can't!

*M Russell*

## CONVENT CARS

Mouth was stretching hard and red
Lying on her tarmac bed.
Caustic breath. Hair brushed higher.
Skidding with pleasure, blood tasted tyre.
Lips met windscreen. Eyelids flick
In the cold congealing sick.

The great acrobat drove the crowd
Hooting. Bleating. Meating loud
To see her skin twisting taut
Tearing the body she'd recently bought.
Body. Sexed up. Flailing
On the glass where she's impaling.

The kerb-crawler had had his way urgently
Sucking. Fucking. Mucking up fervently.
Then came the white-coats. A liver to lick
They fingered hermetically before the public
A life was ingested then spat on the floor
Virginal subject became objectified whore.

Zipped past the neck in a black rubber number
She wheeled to the lights, unaware in her slumber.
Hair caught and salted. Flavoured. Tin-tainted
Teeth chipped and torn in the face, freshly painted.

Men pulled their flies. Women their necks
As the breathless, second-skin beauty finally had *sex*.

*Sarah A Lucas*

## WHAT ARE YOU ON ABOUT?

Am I laying by a riverside
Or am I drifting through the sea?
Am I looking by myself
Or is it you watching me?

Am I speaking an unknown language
Or are we conversing a million words?
Do we know each other anymore
Or am I just being Absurd?

*Lawrence Savage (17)*


## SEA BIRDS

Out on his arm she swung like a charm,
Twisting and dancing and shouting with glee.
The river, she cried, I'm a frog, I'm a sail,
I'll swim 'cross the creek, I've the wind in my tail.
I'll beat you to Kent, though your are the male.
You won't he replied, come along, thought you do
Have your yellow suit on with edging of blue.
Purply spots, are they really the thing?
You look like a dish-rag hung out on a string.
I've invented a boat, and to give it its due
The cut of its jib is much better than you.
Sleekly it runs, and don't answer back,
I've had quite enough of your saucy chit-chat.
Why, beat me to Kent, at the turn of the tide
I'd beat you to Margate, well, maybe not quite.
They forced their way through with cleaving arms two,
And punished the water for being so blue.
Their quarrel was ended , for drying on shore,
They hadn't the strength to row any more.

*Hazel Heasley*

## HEAVEN OR HELL

How can a feeling such as this be transformed,
Into such dull things as words?
What language is there to encompass the surge,
And decline of this maelstrom?

There is nothing which can compare,
With that heart-stopping moment,
Between the desire and the kiss.

That second that the eyes meet and understanding flows.
Then the hurtling, slow-motion plunge into an embrace.
A kiss as light and fleeting as déjà vu and there,
The incandescent heat of realisation and a moment is created.
More precious than a sunrise,
Yet lasting and solid as a breeze.

Then the mounting tide,

The pressure of a million wonderful possibilities,
And one dark, agonising instant filled with the fear of rejection.
Or, worse still, the hacking stab of laughter.

Then a smile, shared, warm enough to melt the ice in the glasses.
A sigh and the gentle thundering of the heart,
Disturbed only by the infantile giggle of Cupid,
And the receding flutter of wings.

The arrow finds its mark.

*Martin Fitt*

## BITTER SWEET

What beauty can be seen in Winter's cold hard face
Those leafless trees appear as though being made of lace
Each season bringing with it much glory and much charm
Even icicles and ice cold rain never do much harm.

Reluctant sunshine filtering through the trees
The exhilarating air with more than a hint of breeze
Feathery clouds floating with great splashes of grey
And so begins another Winter's day.

Beautiful children hurrying to school
Cosily wrapped in scarves and overcoats of wool
The quicker to escape the winds and freezing rain
In their hearts wishing they were home again.

The early morning bright with frost which will glisten
And oft times to birds' songs we try to listen
The whistling wind through the branches bare
Snowflakes threatening to fill the air.

That wanton air - so crisp and clean
Promise the coming Seasons to be more green
But hills of snow above in the skies
Promise another view of Paradise.

*I Fox*


## CONFUSION

The autumn sky is approaching
Nothing seems real
I'm sitting here alone
Wondering what it is I feel
Is it the first time I kissed you
When summer was wild and alive
Or is it the death of the dream
Like a wound open wide?

The mystery keeps hanging
Like a cloud over my head
I thought I knew who you were
But I haven't ever met you yet
Every time I see you
You're wearing a different face
You change like a chameleon
But never leave your space.

I remember you in white like a virgin
In the strange glow of the room
Before the towers of time went crashing
And left us both staring at the moon
Now the days all bleed into one
And the night is just an ache
It feels like this is the end
But all I can do is wait.

*Philip Craigie*


## SEEING - YET BLIND

The beauty of the earth with the rising sun
Is taken for granted as day is begun.
The hustle and bustle of nature's life
Is drowned by the sounds of man's constant strife.
The ever-changing skies go passing by
Quite unnoticed by you and I.
We seldom see a leaf fall from a tree.
For we are blind in a world which can see.

*C J Gaskin*

## RELATIONSHIPS

Pain, suffering, hurt
Close the door
Shut it tight
Bar it and bolt it
To nurse your wounds inside, alone
As a wounded animal
But that way lies death
That way lies festering
Not healing
No, leave the door open
If only a chink
Where light and air may come in
And slowly
Almost imperceptibly
It will open
On new horizons.

*Rose Sefton*


## HOUSES OF PARLIAMENT

A building standing tall and proud
Built by man, that shouts out loud
These stones are laid with loving care
Planned and drawn with thought and dare
Upwards outwards on they go
Windows, turrets what a show
Statues, gargoyles take their turn
To stand in line their faces burn
As sun shines through and strikes on them
A burning glory turns boys to men
So as they sit to plan our fate
And we outside just stand and wait
It's the Houses of Parliament
        Magnificent

*B M Eels*

# FRAGRANT MEMORIES

Of all the English counties
The one I love the best
That stirs the deepest feelings
In an exile's breast
The country lanes, the cottages
With roses round the door
The rippling streams, the babbling brooks
All these I do adore.
Sandy beaches, pinewoods and windmills
Softly turning,
Standing out 'gainst Norfolk skies
Set my heart a-yearning.

A gentle breeze caress my brow
And fragrance fill the air,
As skylarks soar and sweetly sing
O'er lavender fields so fair,
Do not forget the poppies proud
Scarlet and full of glory
They also have a part to play
In this Norfolk story.
Yes, my heart is still in Norfolk
For I am Norfolk bred
But now I live in Suffolk
I must make that do instead.

*Jennifer Ashman*

## SUBURBAN CHILDHOOD, 1930S STYLE

The streets of my childhood were clean and empty
With municipal trees at municipal paces apart,
And clipped privet hedges, and fences and gates
To three-foot deep front gardens
To keep the neighbours out and the families in.

Come straight home from school, never stay to play in the street.
Find your friends within the family circle.
Go out? Go for a nice walk.
Go to church on Sunday, wearing hat and gloves.
Always hat and gloves. Respectable.
Appearance is what matters. What if it is all surface, nothing beneath?
Say: Good morning, Vicar. Smile at vaguely-recognised faces
Which smile back.
Names? No idea. Maybe they live in the same street.
But we don't mix. We keep Ourselves to Ourselves.

Single-sex school. Of course.
Do your homework. Get a scholarship.
Go out? Join Guides. That's single-sex.
It's attached to the church. It's respectable.

Like our lives. Clean. Tidy. Empty. Respectable.
Never mind how empty, how meaningless.
Respectable. That was what mattered. That was the buzz-word.
(but they didn't call it that)

And now we are *alive* and *respectable* - has it any meaning now?

*F Jones*

## THE PHOTO ALBUM

One rainy day a little old lady
Sat on the sofa with grand daughter Sadie,
And old family album upon her knee
Spread out flat for the girl to see.

Most of the photos were faded and old,
But she listened intently to all she was told.
They looked at weddings and bundles of joy
Sprawled out on cushions 'Who's that baby boy?'

'That girl on the seesaw - she looks so glum'
'Oh, don't say that dear, she's your Mum!'
Over we go, more frills and lace,
And what a pretty little face!

Asked Sadie, 'Who on earth is she?'
'Aha!' said Gran, 'Guess who? It's me.'
Then all of a sudden something fell out,
And quick as a flash the child gave a shout.

Snatched up an old photo and had a quick look,
'Oh, soldier. Nice man,' put it back in the book.
But the little old lady was lost in time
Reliving the rapture of moments sublime.

So there they sat, the young and the old.
But the old one's secret will never be told.

***Winifred Rudderham Baker***

# CALLED UP IN THE 40'S

The number they gave me along with a gun
Was One Nine One Seven Four Three Seven One,
Learn and remember it that's how you are known
You are just a number now and the army's your home,
Your country's at war you will fight and defend
The freedom of living, though some lives will end,
To achieve this goal of freedom for all
We laid down our tools and answered the call,
We marched up and down until we were spent
We all knew the drill sergeant wasn't a gent
By the orders he gave, the words that he used
He made our ears ring with his verbal abuse,
Get your hair cut, get a shine on those boots
While we just stood still like a squad of dumb mutes,
But six weeks of this turned us into a soldier
It made our hearts harder and our bodies much older,
The rifle, the kit bag became part of our lives
But we knew in our hearts only the lucky survives,
But now looking back you forget all the bad
And remember the good times and pals that you had,
But the number remains it is etched on your brain
You hope never to want it never again.

*C R Hollman*


# THE MIRROR OF TIME

The mirror of time does not lie
But reflects what it sees at a glance;
The image it gives is the truth,
No appeal, no deceit, no fresh chance.

It may catch us when quite unaware,
The identity real and exposed;
In a flash we may hide from the truth
With a smile that remains quite composed.

The impersonal mirror of time
Will not show compassion or hope,
But only the rush of the years
And a future that's vague and remote.

Then hasten away while we can
From the stories we read from each line;
For the mirror reflects what has been
And the future's not ours to define.

*Vanda Gilbert*


## MORNING GLORY

Still orange morning,
Day wakens for the dawn,
Dark skies leave the horizon,
And the new day has been born.

In the glow of morning light
We can see the work of Jack Frost,
Come, leave your beds to witness
Its beauty before it is lost.

He has sprayed the trees and hedgerows
With a coat of glistening white,
As if he sought to override
The darkness of the night.

Diamonds strung across corners,
Where spiders' webs are spun,
Soon the warmth of daytime
Will have his work undone.

And sleepyheads who never wake,
'Till after the day has begun,
Will never know of the beauty
That was there before the sun.

*Margaret Burgess*

## WE HAVE AN EARTH

We have an Earth
it's a wonderful place
the sun is our light
and the rain is our grace
We have an Earth

We have the soil
with which we provide
all of the good food
we put down inside
We have the soil

We have the people
to provide for our needs
to care and to tender
among other good deeds
We have the people

We have the spirit
to endure pain and sorrow
we have the foresight
to plan for tomorrow
We have the spirit

We have a vision
to end all the wars
to stamp out the greed
and whatever it cause
We have the vision

We have an Earth
it's as round as a ball
its bounty is plenty
and enough for us all
We have an Earth

*G W Hubbard*

## TO GARETH

Dreams are hard to reach
Most give up before the start,
But you, have reached the second base
Don't stop now.
I know you can make fourth,
You feel like you've lost friends?
No, they weren't friends,
Only agents sent to break you,
I don't believe you're wasting time
Just sowing your seeds,
You'll smile when you look back
At the many soul seeking nights
'Cos you'll be able to say
They were worth every hour missed,
Each night you're closer
To your special dream,
You know you can make it,
Sit back,
See the reality around you,
Feel it,
You've touched the inspiration,
Now grab it,
You're singing in the right key,
The hard work will be repaid
Just stick around to see.

*Joanne Cooke*

## THE GYPSY MAN

The gypsy man, he laughs at me,
He wished me death for eternity,
'Twas mesmerised within my soul,
To fall in our earth's dark black hole.

I stepped into a crystal grave,
I burnt my lips upon the devil,
Heavy heart like stones of a falling cave,
I slipped down to his level.

I tore the clouds and the rain apart,
I saw old faces without a heart,
I heard their voice when they looked at me,
And gave directions to their fantasy,
The blindness of society.

Now before me, I see, heaven's gate,
It's shut and locked by God's own hate,
I turn to face eternal grief,
No hope left for this crumbled leaf,
Yet, this ends my drowning faith

Now fall the angels with broken wings,
With tortured tears for my forgiveness
They sing,
So tell me God, is this the rain
to sprinkle life on me again?

*K M Piccoli*

## PICTURE OF YOU

If I could paint a picture
it would be of you
I wouldn't paint the way you look
because you look so blue
With lots of colours your face
would come alive
Instead of looking old and grey
you would look twenty five
Your grey eyes I see every day
would be the deepest blue
I'd put colour in your cheeks
that's what I would do
I just couldn't paint the face I see
it would sadden me so
I'd paint colours in your face
that would make it all aglow
And after when it was all done
and I could see your happy face
I'd put it in a frame and trim it
with pure white lace
Then hang it on the wall
where I could always see
Your lovely smiling face
smiling back at me.

*Linda Roberts*

## OUR FINE CITY

How often do you hear someone say -
'I think I'll go down the city today'
But they don't know what fun awaits
Within our own familiar gates.

First to get there, please don't fuss
Just because they've changed the bus -
And the route is not the same
It's just the bus company's latest game.

So as you ride down Magdalen Street
And you can hardly keep your seat -
And later when you feel those bumps
Blame it on those traffic-calm humps.

If you have time to spare at all -
You really must visit Castle Mall
The shopping's good there is no doubt
It's just a problem getting out.

If next it's a book that you need to return -
Then there is something you must learn -
It's no good having worn out feet
'Cos the library's now in Ber Street.

You're feeling weary - your head aches
You'd like to sit down with tea and cakes
The Assembly House - it cannot be
After the fire, there's not much to see.

But with all these pitfalls to bring us down
It's not really such a bad old town
At least the tourists think it's a hit
And we Norwichians just love it!

*Patricia Rowell*

## A RARE SUMMER'S DAY

A rare summer's day
When the east breeze is warm.
And down to the beach
The day trippers swarm
They come laden down
With windbreaks and beds
Sunfactor sixteen
And hats for their heads.
But once settled in
Caution's thrown to the air
As everyone bares
As much as they dare.
Children run naked
Across golden sand
And scanty clad lovers
Stroll hand in hand
Three OAPs
Braving the sea.
Skirts hitched up high
Paddle up to their knees.
Lunch time at last and
They gather to eat
Their sand-dusted picnics
A sumptuous treat.
Who needs foreign shores
When England can boast
Such wonderful scenes
On her own East Coast.

*Denise Amis*

## THE FALL FROM HEAVEN

The blood dripped for all of us -
All round the body, on a cross;
The super-normal body that stands
Around the streets of heaven.
Pure spirit of love eternal and invisible,
It doesn't decay and attract flies.
Unlike the blackberry bush
in which the Devil fell when he came crashing down.
The Prince of Lies was kicked out of
Heaven for his haughty claims.
'I will be the life and the death for man;
they will worship only me'.

The black juice ran down his horns
It mixed with his purple blood.
His screams summoned the demons and elementals
No time to be sentimental, they used all the power of darkness.
Pull the Devil from the briar and
we will light a fire.

The fire got out of control
And the ground split and they all fell
down deep to the bowels of the earth.
The fire, the Devil and all the army
of hell fell into the eternal pit of fire.
Over it grows the blackberry briar.

*Nicholas Lake*

## THE FOX

His eyes gleam
The soft silky fur reflecting the sun
Trotting on the soft green grass
he lies down to rest.
Silence.
Then,
That dreaded sound
The hunter's horn.
Picks himself up.
Running like the wind
Turn this way, that way
Try to lose the hunter, the dogs
The barking of the dogs
Closer, closer and closer.
he doesn't run fast enough.
Growls - howling.
The silence again
All around.

*Brooke Westerman  (13)*


## THE SWAN

So graceful upon the water are they
Adults of white and cygnets of grey
On ponds and rivers they are to be found
And very often on sandy dry ground
The Mute, the Bewick and Whooper who
Are European and British too
With feathers which are so clean and bright
When preening can last long into the night
We are so proud of these birds on the lake
Such a pleasant sight to the eyes they make
The swan is beautiful and so very fine
So fishermen beware of lead on your line.

*Anne Galloway*

107

## MY CHILD

We walked in the fields, then came the hounds,
She clutched my hand, alarmed by sounds
That tore and slashed at calm spring air,
We watched as the stag with bursting heart
Rolled neck over crop and played his part,
We watched the tortured breathing cease,
I saw his death - she saw his peace.

We strolled on the green, then came the din
As kids tore from school and tried to win
The prize for biggest shriek and dare,
They found the yokel unaware.
With cries of glee they ringed their prize,
Blew scraps of dust into his eyes.
They spun him round and back again,
I saw his laugh - she saw his pain.

We walked through the wood as evening fell,
We felt the magic of the dell,
Then glimpsed the ragged poacher still
Behind the tree, we sensed the ill
That he would do to some poor mite,
But could not move to help its plight,
We saw the cruel cudgel rise,
Smash furry head with startled eyes,
I cursed him and the ground he trod,
But she saw his need - and I saw God.

*Fred Sampson*

## WHO DONE IT

I like to read a mystery
'Bout who done what and when,
Could be mistress could be wife
or even Uncle Ben,
The wife is suspect number one
Who did this dirty deed,
She had the motive and the knife
'Twas jealousy and greed
The mistress could have done him in,
And caused this awful strife,
her lover had just told her
he wouldn't leave his wife.
Uncle Ben's the culprit,
At least that's my belief,
He tried to steal the jewels
Was just a common thief.
He made a bungle of the job,
A fiasco from the start,
Got disturbed and panicked
Stabbed his victim through the heart.
I try to solve each mystery
Before the guilty one's revealed,
it makes me feel quite clever
To know who's fate is sealed.
Sometimes, if I'm not too smart
I cheat towards the end.
And turn the pages just to see
Who the police will apprehend.

*Margaret Malenoir*

## HOW ARE THE MIGHTY FALLEN

Down in the woodland, blow after blow,
There, where the giants of the forest grow.
Fascinated I stood and glanced,
Towards a gap where the grey smoke danced.
Among the pines I loved and knew,
There were the giants of the forest grew.

Faintly borne on a playful breeze,
Ghosts of men, whispers of trees;
A mighty blow, a sickening thud,
I could imagine the sticky blood,
Oozing sap which slowly dropped
Where many branches had been lopped.

I could imagine a prince of pines,
Amid his peers in the fallen lines,
Where many another age-old tree,
Had rested at last on a mossy sea,
His cones and needles most softly shed,
Another giant of the forest was dead.

*Mary G Lundberg*


## HARVESTING AT UNION FARM

The sun is blazing, the heat is intense.
The horses are working.
Harvest time is here.

Bustle and noise of men and horses,
Working together in the fields.
Cutting and stacking,
Wheat they are packing,
Making a haystack fit for a king.

Now it is finished,
The horses are resting.
Celebration of the harvest is here.

*Rose Baines*


## SUNDAY TEA

Before these days of watching weights and counting every calorie,
The highlight of our week was Sunday tea.

A tablecloth of linen, dazzling white,
Dainty china, glinting bright,
Silver a'gleam in the warm firelight,
That's what we loved to see!

Golden butter, thickly spread
On crusty slices of home-baked bread,
Jams and jellies, orange and red
And giant pots of tea!

Currant tea-cakes, lightly spiced.
Fruit cake rich and royally iced,
Ham, so pink and neatly sliced,
That was the fare for me!

Chutney, pickles, pies of pork
Celery crisply white of stalk,
So much to eat, no time for talk
At any Sunday tea!

Before these tedious diets for the slimmer shapes we seek,
Sunday tea, at four o'clock, was the highlight of our week.

*Joan Brocklehurst*

## TO HELL OR NOT TO HELL

Scream at the sun
Wail at the wind. Forever
Our souls will lie
Wicked. We sinned
Claw at the clouds
Reach for the rain
We'll spend our death-time
In Devil's domain
Weep for the wings
That would take us above
Pray for the peace
That we yearn for and love
Cringe at the cruel
Deeds that we've done
Moan at the misery
Caused by our fun
Scorching our skins
As we're pulled down below
For your sake be good. Or
You'll suffer. We
Know.

*S K Cooper*


## THE DAFFODIL

The daffodil may come and go,
Time to give a glancing glow,
Yellow mist upon the lawn,
Buds of spring will soon be born.
Bright soldiers round the leafless trees
Brings nature's chill to its knees.
Takes Jack's claws from icy blast,
Life begins and smiles at last.

*Stephen G Betts*

## ON DYING

When my turn is come my dear,
I'll gather all my memories,
Would you, just one last time draw near
And tell me how it really is.
Hold my hands to form a chain
And if you need to, cry some tears
And then let's deal with all the pain,
let's go back over all the years.
let's put to right, harsh words we spoke
And speak the ones we left unsaid.
Let's clear the tangled weeds that choke,
Then truth can bloom around my bed.
And when the hurt is all put right,
I'll go in peace, to meet the light.

*Lyn Ellis*


## YOU ARE

You are dawn's early glow
You always give to others,
The warmth and brilliance of the sun
That you radiate to one and all,
The sparkling feeling, when all is fresh
And lovely after showers,
The colour and fragrance of flowers
That fills our lives with joy and beauty,
Then at sunset the hush and calm of sweet contentment,
You are all of these dear Eileen.

*Elsie Betts*

113

## CREATION

Far as the eyes can see
It seems from here to eternity
So lucky! To be free.

To walk and feel the gentle breeze
The love of nature all around
As we tread God's given ground

Alas! Sometimes there's not a sound
Because of folk who hunt and hound
It would be good to see again
Creatures happy on the plain
Free from taunt and pain.

To feel the fresh clean rain
Descending from a clean fresh air
That's good to feel and breath
Happy, without a care,
With nothing to despair.

Far as the eyes can see
Beauty of hills and trees
Appreciating all of these
I do a step and click my heels
It's so good to be alive!

As I look around, and see
All the things, God's given me
Not just me, but everyone
All creatures under the sun.

To live and share together
For always and forever
Showing appreciation
To a beautiful creation!

*Margaret Edwards*

## THE HOMECOMING

It had seemed a good idea, when he rode away to war,
And if thought of his return at all,
        It was as 'Things to be how they were'.

But now the crusader rides home from afar,
To find the moths have feasted
        for seven winters on his robes of fur;
Home to a dying heir and barren wife,
With an old wound and a new grief.

His heart, which had pranced like a young doe,
In a green wood, on a spring day
Was as dour now as a debt due
On a losing throw with a false die.

It had seemed a good idea when he rode away that June,
But where was the joy on his return?

*Joseph Mason*


## WINTER'S ENCHANTMENT

Jack Frost breathes his gentle breath:
Across forest and moor,
into lake and pond:
He spreads his cloak of brilliance
over this naked barren land;
creating a winter wonderland,
enchanting a sleeping countryside,
waking it, momentarily, from its yearly slumber;
with a beauty that matches the colours of spring,
a freshness that substitutes the fragrances of summer,
a magic that brings a moment of life
to a snow-white serenity.

*Tara Jane Scriggins*

## MOUSEHOLD MEMORIES

Oh lovely Mousehold with its valley and hills
They say the air up there will cure all your ills
There's heathers and ferns bushes and trees
Quite a delight for your eyes to see

What wonderful days when we were young and carefree
Up there we would go and take our tea
After fun and games and a lot of laughs too
We would all shout 'Hooray' when that factory horn blew

As we could then eat our sandwiches and have a cup of cold tea
We were so happy my friends and me

As we grew older to the bandstand we would go
To listen to music of long long ago
And to meet up with boyfriends and hope for a date
For a night at the pictures *Clark Gable* was great

Then we would go a courting hand in hand
Over the hills wasn't life grand
Yes many a tale number nine bush could tell
Up there on Mousehold I remember it well

*E Atkins*


## DEEP WITHIN

Race colour creed,
You need to look inside indeed.
To find the truth, of warmth and love,
These are the words of God above.

Why judge at what our eyes do see,
It is inner tenderness and care, the truth be.
So much hatred in this, our world.
Just because real thoughts are held.

116

Like sheep one follows the first shout,
Get that alien out.
If only one would follow one's own mind,
Then it would be, a shout of a different kind.

For the rough and tough are really small,
It is the ones that follow, that makes them tall.
So look not to colour of the skin,
Look deep now, to see what is within.

And there you will find what is truly meant,
And all live in harmony peace and in content.
Made in God's own image all are we,
So it is up to us, to live contented wise and with serenity.

*V M Foulger*


## DAMSEL IN DISTRESS

We thought we'd lose her, burning to the ground,
Sly vandal fire, sparking without sound.
Scorching smoke and flickering flame,
Urged the question - who was to blame?

From the town a gathering crowd,
Stood in silence, heads sadly bowed.
Poor old lady, consumed by heat
As firemen battled against her defeat.

Blackened, charred, a tangled mess.
Experts pondered, then had to confess,
They didn't know - was she beyond repair?
Spectators waiting groaned in despair.

But favoured fortune smiled like before,
Re-building started from the seashore.
And Southend people gave joyous cheer,
For back again was their longest pier!

*Elaine Hutter*

## WHO WANTS TO BE A WITCH?

Witches must be stupid, completely off the rails
If we believe in all those superstitious tales
Taking frogs and human hair and even dead men's eyes
Yuk! Fancy mixing all that lot when making all your pies
It's enough to make you ill so I'm sure it can't be true
And when you go shopping don't you wonder at that queue
That's the witches buying groceries, well half the queue at least
And when you look into their trolleys what a lovely feast
There's steak and bacon and rice and bread
With yoghurt and butter, you can see they're well fed
Dancing round the bonfire in the dead of the night
When you come to think of it, it isn't very bright
Whether in the snow or rain, or just extremely cold
Anyone who attempts this must be extremely bold
Just imagine all that frostbite on fingers and on toes
And when it comes to chilblains, blue everything goes
Surely if it is that cold they would warmly dress
Wearing all their winter clothes including thermal vest
If this, for a witch, is what it's supposed to be
I'm surprised they don't spend all their time watching their TV
They could be knitting pairs of socks, or even doing cross-stitch
'Cos if that's what you have to eat and do, who wants to be a Witch?

*Sonia Gillings*


## NORFOLK SUMMER

Scarlet poppies, gleaming in the fields
Of wheat and barley;
While in the hedges, wild roses bloom
With many varied hues, from palest pink to deepest rose.
High in the sky, swifts, twisting and turning,
And over streams and meadows
Dart the swallows.

The keen-eyed hawk hovers, watching, waiting,
Suddenly, he falls down, down, into
The long grasses to find his prey.
The cattle quietly graze on the marsh
And sheep crop the grass on gentle slopes.

Meadowsweet and rush in flower,
Buttercups and on the millpond
Kingcups bright;
Long grasses, swaying in the gentle breeze;
What better place to be
Than Norfolk, in high summer.

*J Harrison*


## FANTASIA

East Anglia
My fantasia
Sunny Days
Land that pays
Chocolate box scenery
Breaks without misery
Lots of walks
Endless church talks
Tree lined views
Local news
Places to stay
Fields to play
Pine trees galore
And much much more
In East Anglia
My Fantasia

*Cherry Somers-Dowell*

# THE DESTROYER

Near to the answer
I search for food to fill the hunger of my mind,
Thirsty for thoughts of unknown reason
I travel far and wide.

The streets are bare, the night is cold and I see
a lonely traveller standing amidst the cold and dark,
Curiously I move close, searching his mind,
scanning his thoughts to see if his are unknown.
But no, no luck,
I must press on else I shall wither away.

Floating over grass and ground I search for a weary prison
of life,
ready to give his mind of unknown thoughts to me,
to become free of trouble and strife.

Drop by drop I fall
to the softening earth beneath me.
Feeling the touch of air surrounding me,
enclosing my ever curious self.

For I am destroyer of unknown souls,
Surviving on them,
Weeping if none are found,
But as I weep my spirit weakens,
Leaving the night to defend for itself,
for the stronger souls destroy me.

***Deborah E Guddee***

## THE SPORTING 90'S

Sporting victories were many in this present decade
Medals were won and new records were made
Our golfers excelled on the fairways and greens
With birdies and bogies - whatever that means!

. . . And then we lost a cricket match

Will Carling led England's rugby team a Grand Slam to win
Stephen Hendry won trophies when he dropped the black in
The Nation's football manager changed yet again
We won some and lost some but did well in the main

. . . And then we lost a cricket match

Mansell and Hill raced cars to win the Grand Prix
Our oarsmen rowed boats to gain victory
Chris Boardman flew round the track on two wheels
Whilst our runners and jumpers had wings on their heels

. . . And then we lost a cricket match

Ice skaters bowed out, tennis players retired too
And our hockey teams showed just what they could do
World records were broken all over the place
When Steven Backley's javelin was launched into space

. . . And then we lost a cricket match

South African sportsmen are competing once more
And proving they're just as good as before
Kenya's cross country runners we just couldn't catch

. . . But England finally won a cricket match!

*Angela Morley*

## NOBODY

Tattered clothes hang from her gaunt frame
once designer labels belonged in her wardrobe
now her worldly goods she holds in a Sainsbury's bag
once she had a loving and caring family
but take a look at her now.

Begging on the streets, every penny counts
one cup of tea, makes the day more bearable.
Drink and cigarettes, dull her thoughts
Cold hard pavement, her bed and board
Once she had a home of her own.

A society that no longer cares
all she is, a number, not even on a list
no job, no home, no home, no job
all she is yesterday's news, a nobody

She is forty, going on seventy
her hollow eyes, show her pain
she sees the people rushing by
ignoring the tramp with her hand held out
once she had believed, she was someone

Everyday dramas go on around her
drug dealing, fights, prostitution
all these things, she had once despised
now it's all part of her daily life

She had pride a long time ago
now all she can do is haunt the streets
down and out, at home, in Cardboard city
Seven long years without a job, has brought her here
once she had a decent future, and hope
but take a look at her now.

*Jane Fairweather*

## IF LIFE IS A BOWL OF CHERRIES, WHY AM I SUCKING ON A KUMQUAT?

I live in a world where there are no surprises,
Where nothing is unexpected.
I was born in a storm with a slap and a cry
Then my face was stamped *rejected.*
So I hide behind a despondent mask
That carries a blank expression.
I'm wearing a new cologne today,
Do you like it? It's called *Deep Depression.*
My conversations wither, awkward
Silences ache to bloom,
I'm married
I'm married to the blues
And she fills my life with gloom.
I sleep on the streets of sadness,
I cross the paths of woe,
I'm quickly going nowhere because
I've go nowhere to go -
Except Hell and Purgatory
Where Dante's Inferno awaits,
(He burns your passport as you enter
Then turns and locks the gates).
Hope is a dirty, four-lettered word,
Bliss is beyond repair,
I'm paranoid and lonely,
Fed on fear, frantic with despair.
Perpetually stuck under a dark cloud
In a mac with a leaky brolly
I'm the last Bohemian of misery
And my name is Mel - Melancholy.

*Jason Raper*

## PETTICOAT LANE

Clockwork pigeons, early morning market,
drowsy eyed people, down at heel.
Shabby grey harridan, mingles with scavengers,
unseen, unloved, what does she feel?

Frayed and musty, wrinkles and grime,
astrakhan coat, worn out shoes.
Hunting through myriad, second-hand, treasure-trove,
bony fingers, so eager to choose.

Blue satin party dress, held to the sky,
thin arms shake, shiny threads gleam.
Untold memories held in bright cobalt eyes,
time eclipsed by a passionate dream.

In stunned silence I see vivid beauty before me,
vibrant eyes, young, though years have slipped by.
Gossamer fabric of joy and pain,
love once known . . . undimmed by time.

Clockwork pigeons, early morning market,
drowsy eyed people, down at heel.
Shabby grey harridan, mingles with scavengers,
unseen, unloved, what does she feel?

*Linda E Delgaty*


## I WOULD

Yes, I could live, without you.
I could live without a lot of things.
The mind looks after itself,
Gaping holes are filled or forgotten.
Eventually, I would probably go for weeks without
a thought of you.

But now
I am full of you.
I spend my days with you
or the absence-of-you.
Together time is sharper, more colourful,
I hurt more, I am more.
Your essence has changed mine
but showing itself to me.
Your offerings become precious -
a bottle-top, a conker,
a smile.
You make me happy
by being in the same room as me,
But yes, I would live, without you.

*Fiona Hall*


## PRAYER FOR A GREEN BIRTHDAY

This folded prayer with a heartbeat's pledge
Lies now at the foot of the night and day,
Where once, till chance stirred up the storms of fruit
No bud nor blood deserted season bred;
Where no gull's cry had telling of the sea
And mute were the fathoms and fears of love;
Where stars bloomed blind which were seed of the sun
And never a shadow had ghost to grieve:

Oh swollen wave that found the spilling tear
And down the milling tides of labour bore
To this impatient sleep the gifted grief;
Deliver not the pledge to squandered death,
Nor cross in vain the reaches of the heart,
Nor leave, when dreams have ebbed, a crooked day.

*Maurice Kelly*

## ON GALLEY HILL

We said grace by the hedgerows,
then, among soft fingers of green
we sat in the morning sun;
reading, eating, speaking of the future
- the feel of an arrow
the armour of years could no longer repel.
Later, high on Galley Hill,
even a scar on the distant horizon
marred not the glory of all we beheld.
On we walked and took to the fields. Hah!
So much for Cartographers:
the map knew paths across the valley
even less than we did - so we made our own.
A voice called my name, and fallow deer
gracefully swept across the field,
running, skipping, hopping,
sometimes stopping for a second,
sensing hounds of admiration
that followed their flight
as they took to their heels once more
- and one of them as black as night.
But among Nature's children
I saw no prejudice that day
high on Galley Hill.

*K C Gooch*


## THE GARDEN OF LOVE

Peace just sits there waiting for us -
Waiting in the garden of love,
It nestles behind the tree of grace -
There in our Heaven Above.

The end of pain, the end of sorrow -
The end of all that is blind
But the beginning of, the new tomorrow -
With all uglyness left behind.

We need fear not, our new world above -
Or dread our time to move on,
As the  sun shines bright in our garden of love -
And the peace, lives on - and - on - .

*Faith Strong*


## INTERLUDE IN NORFOLK

A day for the senses - late November;
A day for awareness of the sky
Bright with the peerless clarity of autumn - dry
With a pale-grey canopy of cloud
Separating over brilliant yellow -
Mellow, but free from mist!
The last brave leaves of the oak
Resist falling, though
Twisting branches know they have to die.

Blue tractors are active, lifting sugar beet.
The low-pitched whirring of machinery
Dominates the field yielding its crop.
No need to stoop and gather; only a few
Mutilated leaves droop on the topsoil.

With hunger not yet sharpened by the cold,
Smooth seagulls glide and coil
behind the slow moving giant.
Compliant with their whim it turns the earth
While they await a bonus from its toil.

*Mavis Scarles*

## BUYING A HAT
(Or Sitting Outside the Hat Shop)

I sat alone outside the store
While Mother did the dealing,
She had to go alone, you see,
But still I have my feelings!

Some boys came running past in front
From school - oh what a feeling
Of freedom when the work is done,
I too have got my feelings!

Then on awhile, while Mother shopped,
Another came to see me;
He was unsteady on his feet
And sometimes almost reeling.

He dropped down to the pavement too
Beside me as a friend,
He talked away, in mutter tone,
I could not comprehend.

I sat quite still and listened on
To new found friend still dreaming,
I wondered what he really thought -
I expect he has some feelings!

'Twas such a shame to see him leave
With faltering steps, still reeling,
Oh that he knew the love I'm given -
How good to know the feeling!

And now at home, at Mother's feet
My thoughts keep wandering back,
To my young friend - he needs some love
To satisfy his feelings!

*Margorie Copus*

## NAGGING

Nag, nag, nag, nag,
all day long.
Nag, nag, nag, nag,
Like a boring tuneless song.
Nag, nag, nag, nag,
have you fixed that shelf for me?
Did you prune that apple tree?
Nag, nag, nag, nag,
you can give the dog his walk,
will you listen while I talk?
Nag, nag, nag, nag,
you can take the kids to play,
she's like a tap that drips all day.
Nag, nag, nag, nag,
did you, mend that broken pane?
She'll nag me now for all this rain.
Nag, nag, nag, nag,
have you cut down all that grass?
I close my mind and let it pass.
Nag, nag, nag, nag,
it started on the day we wed,
and even when we got in bed.
Are you sure you're doing it right?
Hurry up, turn out that light.
Nag, nag, nag, nag,
for thirty years she's nagged non stop,
would someone care to do a swop?
Nag, nag, nag, nag.

*Tom Stockwell*

129

## GOLF RULE 27.2 PROVISIONAL BALL

When on the tee we always strive to have our most exacting drive
But hooks and slices send balls wide and then of course we must decide,
The rules of golf gives us a choice our thinking must be made by voice
*Provisional* the vital word which by our marker must be heard.

Now if we do not make it known the fault is ours and ours alone,
The second ball we send away becomes at once the ball in play
You say the word and play again your course of action now is plain
You leave behind the teeing ground and hope your first ball can be found.

You look around and find your ball so pleased it wasn't lost at all
Your second must be put away because your drive is still in play
Now if you do not play again but forward go to search in vain
With not much time to look around to see if your ball can be found

And then within the time allowed you leave the busy searching crowd
And wander back towards the tee with thoughts that you'll be playing three
But then before you strike your ball you hear that distant welcome call
They've found your ball you breath hooray the first you struck is still in play

Though if before you hear that call you tee and play another ball
Too late that call you have no say your second ball is now in play
The other case is if you stay and search the time allowed away
Five minutes gone return to tee make no mistake you're playing three

The ball you strike is now in play no matter what the others say
Your first they've found just save the cost of that new ball you thought
                                                                    you'd lost
So don't give up that three won't mar your card if you chip in for par
Or put your next close to the pin so just one putt will get it in.

Now golfers often make mistakes and think they're having lucky breaks
Their partners who do not know better don't know the golf rules to the letter
The wise ones number very few the ones who know just what to do
So learn the rules and know with pride that you won't get disqualified.

*S F Barrett*

## TIME

Time is such an endless thing
Who knows what next it will bring
But be sure you are in its hands
As it sweeps its way across the lands
We set our lives by time of day
Working hard, enjoying play
It sets us limits we try to beat
When late for work, dashing down the street
At night time too when having fun
It makes us think of the next days sun
For then it all begins again
And some days time can be a pain
But if you rest and let it by
You'll miss very little, I wonder why
Because in time there is some space
To let you stop and ease the pace
It will soon start up and on you go
You can't resist, it won't say no
But when the time has been and done
And you are struggling it has won
Just look around and ask what for
Do we race time more and more
It always has the final say
Because it rules our every day
We worry when our time is short
And lateness means we might get caught
But one day all this fades away
As we grow old, with a shorter day
And then time says to all of us
Hop on board, it's your last bus.

*M S Comer*

## VJ DAY - TWO MINUTES SILENCE

The clock strikes the hour
The silence begins.
Tears trickle down a wrinkled face
Tired and worn.
Returned to another day,
Another place,
No strength then to rejoice,
Little strength now, beyond
A trembling hand,
Two days separated by
Fifty years,
But separated by whom.

It was a lowered head then,
It is a lowered head now.
The line of youth and age
Smudged,
In a silence that hasn't
Yet found its end.

***Alison Bainbridge***


## POETRY

A strange combination of verbs strung together,
To express one's emotionally feelings,
At a given instant in time.

An undiscovered art form,
Highlights unshown talents,
In a varied text,
Fabricating moods,
Darking characters, shading images,
Etching out life.

An embroided tapestry,
In the finest silks,
Illustrating the qualities of vocabulary.

A tacky fraudulent picture,
Shows ignorance,
A lack of language knowledge.

A glossy Vogue magazine cover
Enhances the false props of luxury,
Unneeded for status and glamour.

An odd choice of nouns,
Ends in a mixture of confusion,
Unable to be detangled.

*K Rands*


## SCRATCH OF SILVER

scratch of silver, moved by the breeze
errant thread of spider silk
drifts and lays across her knees
smooth and cream as honey-milk

'I do not love you'            beats my ears
'we can be friends'            my mind reels round
'I love another'              are these my tears
'I think you'll like him'      on the ground

scratch of silver moved by the breeze
lost treasure of some insect ilk
I'd lay my life across her knees
longside a thread of spider silk.

*S T Bacon*

## GOSPEL OAK ROAD

In Gospel Oak, the houses rose
From an incline of a hill.
Their slated roofs reflected sky
On rainy days; our window sill
In carmine red shone bright.
Each terraced house was different
According to the varied taste
Or fortune of each occupant,
And Thirty Three was unimpressive,
But some refinements to it's credit.
A whitened well scrubbed front door step
Defied an unclean foot to tread it
To gain the height to reach the door,
Embellished with a shined brass knob
And matching mirror polished knocker.
It took a while that shining job
To complete with satisfaction,
And in the window whitest lace,
Fresh filigree of mesh, awoke
And shone the unimpressive face
Of Thirty Three in Gospel Oak.

*Val Mansell*


## RECOGNITION

Oh wee animal by the road,
    are you frightened by my load?
        Do you quake as my wheels thunder by
           and giant shapes block out the sky.

Or are you afraid of a nearby foe?
    Is that why your eyes scan the road?
        As you dash out in your escape bid
           perhaps making some human skid.

You are surveying, perhaps with disdain,
    one of the creations of which man is so vain.
        not realising as you count it for nought
            with just how much danger for you it is fraught!

Go back little beast! Go back to your lair,
    for although there may be adversaries there
        Unlike these machines that with indifference pass by,
            Even your foes will pay heed to your cry!

*S Calderbank*


## FORGOTTEN ARMY

Called the 'Forgotten Army', but not by their loved ones you know,
Though the war was now over in Europe, they still had a long way to go,
For they had to fight in the jungle, in the sweltering heat of the day,
And many were captured and beaten, and some with their lives had to pay.
They were tortured and savagely punished, and though they could scarcely
            draw breath,
They were forced by their captors to labour on the terrible railway of death.
They were not the 'Forgotten Army', for though they surrendered their guns,
In our hearts we were right there beside them, for they were our husbands
            and sons
Then we used the ultimate weapon, it was something that had to be done,
At the time there was really no option, were the war to be finally won,
And now that the whole thing is over, we look back with thanksgiving
            and pride
For we know that we owe today's freedom to those men who fought there
            and died.
Here's to the 'Forgotten Army', for though many paid with their lives,
By us they will not be forgotten, for we are their children and wives.

*Rosa Riley*

## SONGWRITING

I'll probably never
create anything
in my life.

And my life will go by,
With the world turning and turning,
But nobody learning a thing about me,
And my pain and suffering
Will all come to nothing.

Except maybe if I could only,
One day, write a rhyme and a
rhythm,
Use the beat as a tool,
Like boys from Liverpool,
Or Brian Wilson,
In his prison.

But I don't want to be on show.
Still, I love music, and
Maybe it can save me
From being another hysteric,
Whinging and pathetic,
Like a girl that nobody
Wants to know.

*Alexis Jeff*


## HELP LINE

The lines so thin, I cannot see,
None out there recognises me,
Hears my plea.
Promises made, hopes matured,
Visions see, studies endured,
Broken word.

Examination undertaken,
Promises mistaken,
Confidence shaken.
Doctors heard,
Not cured,
Broken word.

No future, just past
Fragmented cast,
Teachers Bombast,
Jobs assured,
Jobs deferred,
Hopes absurd,
*No word,*
*No Jobs,*
*No purpose.*

**J Cross**


## ANGLIA ADVERTISER

Anglia Advertiser is the name,
Distribution in all areas is our aim,
VFD circulation that outweighs the rest,
Every Thursday and Friday we send you our best,
Reports from our Editorial teams,
Together with photos that depict the scenes,
Individual help with your requirements,
Situations Vacant to forthcoming events,
Established service with a smile,
Reliable advertiser style.

**Julie Dawn Woolston**

## LITTLE THINGS

A walk in the woods
To see the trees
Kick the leaves beneath your feet
And see the man you've come to meet
He looks and smile at you
because
A smile is quite a funny thing
It wrinkles up your face
And when it's gone
You'll never find its secret hiding place
And far more wonderful it is
To see what smiles can do
You smile at him
He smiles at you
And so one smile makes two.
Then a walk back in the woods
To see again the trees
That's why little things in life are free

*E Fairweather*


## CATS

As sleek as a shadow
Silently padding
Noiselessly pawing the ground.

Gracefully moving
Pouncing and clawing
All without making a sound.

In moonlight a sheen
Is all that is seen
As a movement tugs at your eye.

As mice scamper and scurry
There's no need to hurry
For one of the poor souls will die.

Steel unsheathed
Muscles tensed
The assassin leaps in the sky.

A futile dash
A splatter of blood
And a piteous mournful cry.

The attack abated
The stalker is sated
The hunger inside is fed.

A lick of a paw
And a call at the door
It is time to repose to the bed.

**Simon Ford**

## UNTITLED

Clouds float across the sky
As I wave to you good-bye
The sun begins to set
As it did when we first met
The sky is no longer blue
And I am missing you
The clouds all disappear
And I wish that you were here
The moon begins to rise
My tears I try to dry
Now the sky is black
And you're not coming back.

*Alison Elliott*

## THE WAY OF THE WORD

The way of the word,
To dance with a flair.
To fly like a bird,
To decorate the air.

The word is a present,
And gaudy a jail,
'Tis nil do repent,
The uses which fail.

It laughs like a child,
Lives as a toy.
Masquerades as mild,
Pretends to be coy.

The word is made torture,
To squeeze away life.
To begin an adventure,
With help from a knife.

It is truly insane,
Not literally mad,
The beauty is pain,
That cremates the bad.

The way of the word,
Is that of a maniac
That shoots down the bird,
Then breathes the life back.

*Nina Lemon*

## IMPATIENT QUEUE

An elderly lady
frantically searched
for the correct money,
whilst the bus driver
silently looked on.
Chattering youth and child,
jostled behind her.
With despair,
she burst into tears,
frustrated that Brain
lingered on workout.
A maternal woman,
of eighty three years,
self welfaring,
without state.
School and college eyes
stare without concern.
The tradition of
reverence for age
lost,
along with family life.
So soon, so very soon,
their dancing feet,
whirl into parenthood,
full of losses and gains.
And then suddenly,
it is the impatient queue,
who are fumbling
to find,
the correct change.

*R E A Pugin*

## HEACHAM

It was time to take a break
So we chose to live right here
Knowing the area long before
Brought us feeling of good cheer.

We found it quiet and peaceful
It always was a 'yen'.
Our days are long and happy
As those years roll on to ten.

The lavender fields, a landmark
For they are quite renown
Yes, it's a lively village
Beats living in a town.

To be, it is a nice place
The largest that we know
In the summer it's so busy,
Tourist going 'to and fro'

You get to know the Norfolk folk
With tales that do amaze
Of how this village used to be
In those by-gone days.

We're never lost for visitors
They arrive here by the score
Our house displays a 'Welcome' sign
It's home from home, once more.

*Joyce White*

## THE CALL

One night I saw the moon rise
Over the still, dark sea;
I stood and watched for some moments
Then it beckoned and said to me:
'Come with me upon my journey
And I'll show you the mystery
Of creation, the meaning of all things
From the dawn of eternity.'

I thought for a while as I stood there
On the silent, deserted shore
And the depths of the deep, dark ocean
Sent a message I could not ignore:
'Come with us and see the beauty
That lies in our tender care:
The creatures of day and of night-time
Are waiting to welcome you there.'

Then the moon in its brightness diminished
And shed sparkling tips on the waves
Of the friend it has had through the ages,
Interdependent, the latter with graves
Of the souls who, for whatever reason,
Had answered the silent call
But could no longer visit the moonlight
From the deep, dark depths of the pall.

*Marie Oliver*

## BE MY EDEN

Be my eden,
Fuel my fire.
The garden's beauty,
My heart's desire.

We together are others' loss,
There is a price,
There is a cost,
Tend the garden,
Make it bloom,

Banish the craving,
For ultimate doom,
Tropical birds flash on by,
Reflecting in your loving eyes,

Heart unlocked
The pain floods out,
We are one,
There can be no doubt.

Our loving garden, our paradise lost,
Without you my fire is quenched
We sit upon the wooden bench,

Our glass walled garden,
Plain to see,
But for others it cannot be,
My love for you embraces me.

*Philip Smith*

## MY PARENT'S LOVE

I searched for a love
I thought, I could not find.

The love
my eyes could not see.
which gave life
and has nurtured me.

It has taught me,
to never bow
my head in shame
or to ever runaway.

It has given me
the strength
To never give in.
To live my life
from day to day.

Since first
my eyes were opened
your love has guided
me.

Your love
does not label
or try to make me
something. I cannot be.

Your love
will remain
with me
until I reach
my journey's end.

When my eyes
are closed
again.

*K J Beeston*

## THE SWOOP

Barren branches against a watery sky,
A lonely Hawk with roving eye
Watches the movement of grassy verge
Unconcerned that roadways merge.

A pair of Sparrows, in low flight,
A mating pair; an intriguing sight.
This stealthy hunter, ready to swoop
Circles round then in a loop

In his talons, grasps one of pair
The other left in utter despair.
Hawk soars to sky above
Whilst left behind one half of love.

For the captured little bird
High in the air distress unheard
He knows his end is almost nigh
As he journeys up towards the sky.

His little beak is gasping now,
His weary head about to bow
All blackness is his surround
Whilst mate awaits upon the ground.

She knows her partner is no more,
Yet chicks to feed; they total four,
She'll try her best to make them thrive
And rejoice if just two survive.

She'll hunt for grubs, both morn and eve
Through branch and stalk her way to weave.
When fully fledged, they leave the nest
The skills of feeding put to the test.

Nature's needs to provide
Feeding and killing, side by side
When fully grown to adult life
Faces up to trouble and strife.

*E A Chamness*


## THEY HUNT IN PACKS

They hunt in packs
lingering in shadows
loitering with intent
part of an exclusive brotherhood
the chosen ones
singling out for the cull.
Then moving swiftly
to stick the boot in
to feel the strength of the mob.

After,
they run from the darkness
peeling away from collective guilt.
Each one will tell you it wasn't him,
someone else started it,
self righteous in their denial.
But when fear of discovery has gone,
watch for the knowing glance,
the furtive gesture.
Belonging can be dangerous
and had for another's health

*They hunt in packs.*

*Doreen Russell*

## DINOSAURS AND ROAD SAFETY

Why? Do you suppose Dinosaurs became extinct
Why? Indeed, it certainly makes you think
There were no cars, no roads to cross,
But today the world still mourn their loss
They were very big with giant feet
It was all a game of hide and seek.
If they were around today in town,
It would be all of us who'd get mowed down,
But now it's traffic that causes chaos,
That is if we're not careful how we cross,
Look and listen don't take chances,
And don't pick the middle of the road for your dances,
If it's the red man that means *Stop*
Dare you cross now? That could mean your lot.
Wait for the man to turn to green,
It will be the wisest move you've ever seen.
So if you want to remain alive
Be careful crossing the road and survive

*A Brenda Original*


## INSPIRATION

A gun shoot from nowhere,
A bolt of lightening on a sunny day,
A tear drop from a happy face,
Making sense of confusion.

Light in darkness,
A solitary thought,
A sweet smell of perfume,
The air of success.

Conversion from horizontal to vertical,
A momentary lapse,
A romantic notion,
A strong cry from within.

Ha!

The angry voice of despair,
The scream of pain,
The anguish of hurt.

Where ever it came from,.
It just flats around aimlessly,
Going unnoticed and nowhere.

*K L Rands*


## NIGHT

The pale moon casts its silvery light,
Over the sleeping land,
Twinkling stars in the dark blue sky,
Like diamonds are shining so bright.
Nocturnal creatures begin to stir,
Beneath the woodland trees,
And the eerie sound of a hooting owl
Drifts on the cool night breeze.
The bustle of daytime has faded away,
The night brings quietness and rest,
Long dark shadows cover the ground,
And bats are flying around.
The garden is bathed in a golden glow,
The alley-cat starts to prowl,
The timid field mouse scuttles away,
As the barn owl hunts his prey.
Over the roofs of the quiet town
The beautiful moon shines down.
The hustle and bustle has faded away,
And night ends another day.

*Jenny Porteous*

## AUTUMN

The misty pearly glow of dawning light,
Emerging from the darkness of the night,
Touching the trees of gold and brown
Hung with bright leaves that flutter down,
In the softly sighing breeze,
Stirring the rich beauty of the changing trees.

Oh! Mystic autumn, with your magic view,
Of glorious yellow, bronze, and golden hue,
With sunbeams struggling through clouds of grey
Making each bright and shining ray,
Add to the splendour,
Of the autumned day.

*J Coleman*


## ALL SOULS' DAY

Startled pheasants skitter down the path,
Fields and estuary, sea and reed bed
Draw a darkening horizontal world
beneath the huge wild All Souls sky turned tea-time red.

We are not meant to have perfection long,
Say, just the time it takes going home for tea,
Just long enough so that the common pains,
Reviving, tire us the more with bleak mortality.

So I hope that when we join the multitude,
With palms and snowy robes and all the rest,
We shan't look back on those fields and the glowing sky
And sacrilegiously mutter that that was the best.

*Gillian Judd*

## THE GENTLE MAN

My father was a lovely man
In fact he was a gent
No other dad I'd rather than
To me the world he meant

He had a very handsome face
His hair was dark and thick
He always kept his proper place
Was rarely ever sick

My dad brought up the four of us
Working on the farm
He worked long hours without a fuss
He would do no-one harm

He was a very patient man
He never lost his cool
And he would always understand
He loved us one and all

And when my dear dad passed away
I was there right by his side
And I could only watch and pray
As I sat there and cried

I wish I could have back my dad
Just one more time to see
And then I wouldn't feel so sad
But that can never be.

*D Churchman*

## POETS IN ESSEX

If you want to be a poet not a prat
Go join a poet's circle which will put an end to that!
You'll find that all of them like Shakespeare
You can quote him without fear.
Then, read the lament, by Shelley -
they love to shed a tear!

Pastoral scenes, famous battles, religion,
true love, lost love, the lot!
And, oh boy, what a fascination, death
for some of them has got!
But remember always, what dear old
C S Lewis had to say -
'You'll be lucky if one pair of specs
suits two people anyway'!

Yes, some like humour, some like sadness,
Poets with touch of madness!
So, read your verse in voice so clear -
loud enough for all to hear!
'Til; they sense - 'til they feel,
behind their chairs - those ghostly
Phantoms near!

*Daphne Young*


## MOTHER

Enthroned in her chair
by the window
she would watch
the comings and the goings
of the street;

Sometimes she'd laugh
for no reason that we could see,
but it did not matter
as her laughing made us laugh too.

At other times her brow
would crease in doubt,
or, was it some deep
and unmentioned memory
that she could not put into words?

This,
and the quickness of her mind,
and the humour in her eyes,
and he quiet moments,
made one feel one knew her,
as if one did not know her at all.

*John Brown*


## A WASTED LIFE

The silent scream echoes
Around the warm, safe womb.
Still warm, but safe no more -
Exposed to the world too soon.
Cold, harsh, approached too fast -
Ripped from the haven.
Breathing stopped, a bleeding patch
On the antiseptic table.

*Helen Nicholls*

## LOVELY DAY

I got up this morning, I combed my hair,
I put on my jeans, I began to swear,
I looked out the window and what did I see,
A great big world awaiting for me.
So I ran down stairs for my mail
and my tea, on went my boots and off I'd be.
I took a great big breath of air
I felt as if I hadn't a care.
The sunshine on my face made
me feel so great the world out
hear is such a beautiful place,
I smiled to myself as I went
on my way, no money in my
pocket but a lovely day.
The world was a shining with the
dew on the ground,
The birds were a singing, such
a lovely sound.
So early in the morning, so much
in sight, The wind was a
blowing the sun shining bright
All these things are nature's
way, of making us want to be
part of another day

*Angie Roberts*

## WHISPERS

Look, feel and see
We are part of this world
The world that's too busy
Stop still,
To look, to find.

For in a moment's peace
We pause
We hear the birds
The wild, the sea and its depth.
But not of our mind
Not of our depth

So watch the leaves that rustle
Listen for the tree leaf flutter
Listen!
Listen beyond the breeze
Can you hear the whisper?

So few try
To hear the voice
And less still know the words
Too many things in the way
And so,
Not many listen
And not many learn
Or know
Of the world in the breeze

So still is the mind
The mind that hears the teachings
The mind that hears the whispers

Listen to the whispers in the breeze

*Robert Lomax*

## THE COLOUR OF LONELINESS

Black
I stand silhouetted against an
Orange sky,
Alone in  a world where all colours
Merge and marry
Except
Black
The darkest, most mysterious
Colour of them all
That quarrels with nothing
But matches
None.
Black
The loneliest colour
In a colourful society.
I, too, am black.
But not a shade to be used in
Contrast
My colour has depth and feeling
And a richness foreign to all other
Colours.
When will the various shades
On this vast canvas
Realise that I am of value to them?
That I can, in the hands of a competent artist
Complete the picture of
Humanity.

*Teresa Critcher*

## THE SOLITARY WALKER

A gentle breeze caressed my face that hazy April morning
When I left the bustling village far behind,
Across the undulating fields I walked in solitude
The stress of everyday life removed from my mind.

Further into this tranquil land I strolled
Leaving others to their daily toil,
The drone of a tractor gradually fades away
In the distance, as I leave it tilling the soil.

No mortal or his dwellings are in sight
Just a colourful patchwork of fields all around,
Where the skylark sings her sweet song high above
Whilst the brown hare races along wheat covered ground.

The haze disperses, warm rays of sun shine down
Far on the distant horizon a shrouded edifice revealing,
Where in formation quacking ducks to that sacred place fly,
To Ely, its ancient cathedral the mists no longer concealing.

Are they the souls of my ancestors long departed
Who from those waterfowl, their name did take,
Flying back to their Fenland home, where a living they made
From the land and water, my forbears named Drake.

I must stand and muse no longer, homeward too I must go
Through the set-aside fields I slowly pass,
Where cowslip and purple violet sweetly scent the headland air
Their dainty flowers, now briefly revealed, amongst the grass.

Past a hedge of a million white stars, onward I go,
Where safely concealed chicks await the food their parents bring,
Whilst at its feet the spreading flowering nettle entices the bumble bee
As the sun and sky's reflection in the dandelion and birds-eye, welcome
the spring.

*Sylvia Greening*

## IN MY DARK NIGHT

I knelt in the dark night
My soul taken from myself
My eyes looked
My meaning gone.

For He had taken my soul
And left my body
I, had disappeared
I, could not come back.

How could I endure without my soul.
I knelt and prayed love
Yet I could not come back
So love came and dwelt in me

I shall never be me,
I am dead.
I wept in my loss, in my grief
Now my love is my life
He is me.

*Geraldine Cochrane*


## HAVE YOU EVER STOPPED?

Have you ever stopped and asked yourself why,
One person makes another cry?
Or why one will taunt and tease,
As the other strives to please?

Or why poppies grow and bloom
In a field once filled with gloom?
Why some fought for us and died
As their loved ones sat alone and cried?

It's a strange world with many a different view
Which is the right one, I don't know, do you?

*Melissa Rawlings*

## A CAT CALLED HENRI

We watched him growing old and frail
   and the birds no longer fear,
The function of his tired limbs
   showed the years of wear and tear.
Each time of laying down he'd make
   a whimpering little cry,
As if in pain he'd look at us
   Sad eyes - kept asking 'why'.

His life was long, some fifteen years
   He'd lived with us but four,
We'd loved him, fed and cared for him
   He's with us now no more.
Except to be remembered
   in a *special* sort of way,
He'd slipped from life and pain - to rest
   That mild winter's day.

The Vet had said it was the best
   and kindest thing to do,
One needle prick - one more *meow*
   Then peace and sleep in lieu.
He'd trusted us right to the end
   and we haven't one regret,
For we helped allay the suffering
   Of a truly loveable pet.

He's buried near to his favourite spot
   *Katz Peak* is close where he lay,
He'd been content with his little lot
   and sat there many a day.
Then follow us round as we cut the grass
   or frolic about in the sun,
Our home is quiet now -
   We'll be sad for some time
But we're sure it was right what we done.

*S A Kerrison*

159

## PEOPLE

People lie
A fundamental truth
People die
God - I have no proof
People live
A written definition
People give
In return an expectation
People sleep
Wake up to reality
People weep
Blind by tears they cannot see
People see
But turn a blind eye
People flee
For freedom try
People need
What's yours is mine
People read
Between the lines

*C Jarvis*


## NOT A WONDERFUL WORLD

What a wonderful world, it would be
If nations world-wide could agree
If all wars could then cease
And we could have peace
What a wonderful world it would be

If all weapons of war were destroyed
And scientists, better employed
To make things for a good life
And cut out all bitter strife
What a wonderful world, it would be

But, the world is so full of greed
People want far, far more than they need
They want to excess
Despite others' distress
So, a wonderful world
It can't be.

*R Mitchell*


## HOMESICKNESS

England, oh! England,
Home of my heart,
Dear to the memory,
Now we are apart.
Green fields and Thames grey,
Colours sublime.
Ruby rich sunsets,
Like Last Supper wine.
Soft, sandy slopes, sliding
Into the sea,
Winds of the cold North,
Calling to me.
Hot, crowded underground,
Trains rushing through,
People asleep, on the 6.42.
Fresh fish and chips, as
We walked, Walton's Pier,
Always meant, salt kisses
From you, who are dear.
England, my England,
Let the cottage fire burn,
Ever glowing and welcome,
Until, I return.

*C Beaumont*

## FRIENDS OF THE FOX

Friends, fox and vixen,
Welcome to my den,
Enter please,
And eat my food,
Fear not of any men.

Friends, fox and vixen,
Welcome to my home,
Be comfortable,
And at your leisure,
For no other man shall know.

Friends, fox and vixen,
Bring your children too,
Let them feed,
And their bellies fill,
For no man is seeking you.

Friends, fox and vixen,
Come closer to the fire,
Warm yourselves,
And sleep awhile,
For you're safe from man's desire.

Friends, fox and vixens,
Welcome to my trap,
There's no way out,
Your death is nigh,
For now man will attack.

Friends, fox and vixen,
Bloody, cold and still,
You ran the race,
And paid the cost,
Of man's perverted thrill.

*S Sims*

## WONDERING . . .

Phases of life good and bad,
Some make you happy, some make you sad,
Even from my time of birth,
I wondered, what is my real worth?

I sit by the window and watch the clouds go by,
Wondering, what can achieve if I really try,
Life is a compass full of directions,
Falling in love, making corrections.

People laugh and people cry,
They are so sad, I wonder why,
Is it because they don't know their feelings,
Has it resulted in mischievous dealings.

To forgive someone takes lots of time,
It's almost like serving for crime,
Don't be sad, be very merry,
You will get that final bite of the cherry.

Singing along to my favourite song,
Who cares if I get the words wrong,
Life has no boundaries,
If you're prepared to enjoy it.

Thinking of the love I lost,
I look at my fingers and count the cost,
Have no doubt at all,
I love you.

*Wayne Hudson*

# THE WOMAN I LOVE

The woman I love I made so sad
I long to see her smile
I long to hear her laugh
Oh, how could I have been so bad?

The woman I love is far away
I long to see her
I long to touch her
Oh, will I ever see that day?

The woman I love may love another
Our love is dying fast
I cry all night thinking of her
Oh, how can I be just like a brother?

The woman I love has forgotten my name
My face is fading fast
Our home is just a blur
Oh, how I hurt with pain.

The woman I love knows me no more
My feelings grow stronger
Her feelings grow weaker
Oh, how my heart is so sore.

The woman I love lives another life
Her memory will never fade
I will love her 'til the 12th of Never
Oh, how I wish she were my wife.

*Paul Lee*

## CHILDHOOD REVISITED

Let me look and listen
I know the games you play
it seems I stood there in your place
Only yesterday

Walk along the pavement
Don't tread on the lines
Unheard of things will happen
I recognise the signs

Blow a dandelion clock
Breathless watch those fairies fly
Carrying your wishes
Unto a cloudless sky

Heads bent in childish secrets
Secrets hard to contain
Promise, promise not to tell
Then pass it on again

Running with pure pleasure
Towards an ice-cream stall
A pink? A white? Decisions hard
When you're very small

A bucket and a plastic spade
An architect self-taught
The expert who produces
A palace a moat, a fort

I'm delighted by your antics
Asd you bravely storm the sea
And somewhere amidst your laughter
You hand childhood back to me.

*B Davis*

## IN EARTH

His hair is of the night,
his eyes are of the sky,
Like two dark suns they look down on me crawling along in the earth
The soil is cool and damp.
I bury my ugly face in it whilst feeling his warmth on my back.
I crawl slowly along pulling and straining to travel my journey.
Sometimes I rest from my weary toil and turn on my back, letting his
warm ray shine on my face, drying my tears and warming my skin.
But I turn quickly to the soft darkness when the warmth becomes burning.
All around him the nymphs and goddesses play.
He does not see them, transparent and beautiful, as they fly in his face
laughing and singing.
His eyes are eternally on the earth but the scars on my back are covered
by thin clothing
This is how it will be forever.
he will preside in the sky.
I will be a slave to the earth.
Together we look in the same direction - to the horizon - that mythical
line where the earth and sky finally meet.

*Charley Baird*


## EARTH LIFE

Is the earth ripening or rotting from the core,
Has space travel opened or closed a new door,
Are lessons learnt well or forgotten fast,
And are future flashes a thing of the past,
Who can tell, who do you ask advice?
We need this planet, we need earth life.

What if the ozone collapses,
if another war starts are we ashes,
And if there's no stopping the population explosion,
All acids and chemicals, there's too much corrosion,
Why can't we tell, help, give each other advice?
We all are this planet, we all are earth life.

*Jacqueline Bowden*


## A CONDITIONED SOCIETY

Hunger is a feeling no one desires, but many possess
Depriving a body of comfort and strength,
Taking over the mind, capturing freedom
removing pride, usurping dignity, tormenting the young.
It moves slowly taking one small body over: gradually drying up skin,
wrinkling faces, causing fear and distress.
It licks up any drop of fluid, greedily snatching
at morsels of food till none are left.
Then it moves in for the kill, stalking its prey
like a panther but without the skill or dignity of a fine animal.

Thousands may suffer before the plentiful notice,
notice a country losing everything - its land, its cattle, its people.
We in our surplus
With Cleopatra-like people bathing in luxury

While others have nothing: even less.
Only when we have nothing
will we ever feel what it is like
to slowly die a death
like a zebra torn limb from limb by a lioness.
One minute it's a graceful distinctive beast
the next it's a pile of bones picked at by vultures.

*Caroline Cockell*

## WHERE I LIVE

East Anglia is now the place to be,
The changing weather pattern, you see,
our coast line is next to none,
Having cool breezes so you can enjoy
The sun.

You might choose the golden sand,
Or one of the swimming pools at hand
A walk along the River Yare to see
The oldest drifter for a small fee

Across the water, Gorleston Bay,
Not a pebble golden sands all the way
Cliffs now from the shore line
A walk to Hopton Village find,
A holiday camp along the top,
An interesting church if you have time to stop.

On to Lowestoft, a fish market on quay
Boats unloading plenty to see,
Over the bridge a glass dome, a new attraction
Beach and amusements give satisfaction.

A ride to Dunwich then to Minsmere,
You will find a special birds' sanctuary there,
Alderburgh, a yachting marine,
On the sea shore a delightful scene.

On the way you could stop at Snape,
Benjamin Britten's music makes.
A small piece of East Anglia has been described.
It has been written with genuine pride.

*M Millican*

## MEMORIES OF A COAL MINER

As you light up your fire with a bucket of coal
Remember the men who dug it out of the hole
the men had to work with their pick, their lamp
Hoping walls wouldn't cave in and no pocket of damp
How the air was so foul, littered with dust
For warning of gas to the canary they trust
The lift brought them up when day's shift was done
But oh how much damage had been done to their lungs.

Now you lay a watch as people rush by
Others go on holiday as another plane takes to the sky
Children at play energetically leap around
The milkman trots in and out on his milk round
The paper boy can't stop to shut the gate
his round to do before school or he will be late
The cars speed by others to work must go
Another day comes but life is so slow
For all those who are active and can go anywhere
Remember those who *wish I could* and sit in a chair.

*Evelyn Tomalin*


## MOTHER

Mother, dearest, you're always there,
troubles, laughs, we always share,
If something goes wrong, you're always near,
to make me laugh and show no fear.
'Do unto others' you used to say,
I remember those words, Mum, every day.
Now I'm a mother, and if wishes come true,
then I hope to be a mother like you.

*Joanne Waugh*

## THE DRUNKARD'S LAMENT

Here's to friends, let's raise a cheer
And down another glass of beer,
Forget the banging in your head
Enjoy it now, you're long time dead!
Have a few and act the fool,
Then slide serenely off your stool!
Rising, as the bar spins round
(Head, ablaze, begins to pound)
To hear your drinking buddies shout
'Get 'em in, don't muck about'!
Then head for home in drunken haze,
(You haven't felt this bad for days!)
Crying out in pain and sorrow
*No more ale* (until tomorrow!)

*Robbie*


## FOR DANIEL AND HOLLY

When a flower grows, when the clouds are in the sky,
When a shooting star appears before my eyes;
When the sun shines through, when I hear the raindrops' sound,
When there's stars above, when a leaf falls to the ground.
When the snow falls down, when morning is in sight,
When the sun goes down and daytime becomes night,
When a baby cries, when a rainbow's in the sky,
When the moon shines bright, when a bird goes sailing by.
When a butterfly, unfolds her pretty wings,
When a voice is true and like an angel sings,
When the bells ring clear and when a baby's born,
When the rivers flow, when a breeze is soft and warm.
That's the time I will think of you,
As I think of you, in all that's pure and true.

*Bridget Allen*

## CHARLOTTE

What can I give this child, this daughter of my daughter?
This innocent, who spans the years between us with such ease,
Whose wisdom seems to stem from a thousand years of living,
Who understands my every thought, who looks, and smiles, and sees.

What can I give this child, this daughter of my daughter?
This five year old who gives her granny all there is to give,
One day, maybe, she'll read these lines, this daughter of my daughter,
And then she'll know I give my love, as long as I may live.

*J Ross*


## OVER SHADOW

An emotion deep within me,
Calls upon my fear,
A dark shadowed silhouette,
An outline of rage,
The cortex of your visual centre,
Opens up,
Explaining pertaining sensations,
From the waves.

Understanding *alphas* and *betas,*
pulse exciting
Mind power.

*N F Rushmer*

## LIP-READING

*(For my Grandad)*

Each soul doth have a body
Each sense is dressed on it
To help it on its journey
And in the creator's world to fit.

The eyes serve as a picture
To see beauty all around
The nose serves as a sense
Where fresh baked bread can be found

The skin has a receptor
To allow touch of hot and cold
And the tongue taste the mouth's contents
To see if food is new or old

Our ears serve as a funnel
To channel in the sounds
Of high and low pitched noises
That for eyes are out of bounds.

But some souls, along their journey
Have a lesson to learn from
One sense is lost en route
And it seems one can't go on.

But to make use of other senses
To compensate for loss
Is the best answer to the problem
But another bridge to cross.

So just treat the loss of hearing
As a lesson to learn on
And encourage the other senses
To improve and have some fun.

I hope that with this poem
(because it's where *I've heard* it's leading)
You enjoy your life with another sense
The learned skill of lip-reading!

*N Fleur Tyrie*


## ALONE

As I stand alone,
I think about the past,
What may have been, could have been
If your love for me had last.

I see the laughing couples,
The smiles upon their face,
I compare our love,
To a delicate web of lace.

So delicate, so fragile,
So quick to break,
Just like all the promises,
You used to make.

A tiny drop of rain,
A silent single tear,
Mingle together and fall,
The pain's hard to bear.

A new life begins,
I don't want to be a part,
I want to be isolated
From the hurt in my heart.

The feeling of loss is total,
I know I must decide,
Turn to face the crowd
Or turn my back and hide.

*Dianne Borien*

## IN OUR TOWN (NOT SO LONG PAST)

How peaceful were the streets of our town,
When by 5.30 pm the shops closed down.
Saturday evenings were the best, then folks had come
From not too far not too wide walking, boys and girls
Arrived on cycles for the ride to see and taste
What was on offer.
The prominent venue for meeting friends was
Around the church, before moving off to the
Selected enjoyment of cinema, theatre, summer show or
Roller-skating, maybe down to the prom for just strolling
Fishermen dressed in their Sunday best
Ready to chat with neighbours from outer districts.
Cockles, mussels, whelks and shrimps could be had
Fresh and ripe from a stall to save the appetite.
A school friend of mine would walk along the main street
Accompanied by his four sisters two on either side down
Centre of road to one end then return with no fear of cars driving around.
Later one could buy fish and chips to settle the need
Whilst homeward bound.
Years on these times were referred to as *the good old days*
But were they? Times hard enough for those *in* work.
Comparing life then and now, who were the most contented,
Before so many things had been invented?

*R S Muirhead*


## PAEAN FOR THE ROSE

I once severed a rose in bud
Curled my fingers around its
Green and supple stem -
Pliable thorns caressed my skin.

Ten years on the rose has died
I open my hand to find
A sered brown stem
And cruel thorns to hook my skin.

Mark my path
With beads of blood -
A clew to suppuration
Is revenge for the bud.

*G Dennis*


## CYCLE OF SEASONS

You speak to me through roaring wind
Your tears wash clean my doubtful mind
At night I watch you cross the sky
In wonder through my childlike eyes.
In choirs of birds I hear your song
I dance to your tune all summer long
Mother who satisfies my needs
With love on which my soul does feed.

As summer ends your Green Lord dies
But no tears are shed from your loving eyes
For 'tis only rest that calls him down
He returns again into your earthly gown.
Pregnant with the fruits of your sacred love
You nourish the worlds, both below and above
And when the dark returns and I go within
I will feed from your harvest and learn again.

In the depth of winter the sun returns
Resting no more, of love she yearns
And I will cast off my old life and all of my fears
And call out your name so that all may hear.
In blossoming meadows and in April's rains
New life issues forth breaking winter's cold chains
The cycle of seasons turns again like the moon
The maid of the forest hears again Pan's sweet tune.

*Steven Airey*

## JUSTICE?

Of years gone by I well recall,
Robbery, swindle and theft.
Clever ones who lived by fraud,
Pickpockets so very deft.

To dodge the Bobby on his beat,
Or to cheat the customs, clever.
But to arm oneself with knife or gun,
With a thought to kill, no never.

Life on the Moor, or chance of noose,
Prevailed on us to think.
Weighing the chance of ten foot drop,
With burial in yard of clink.

A Lifer would then serve his time,
Growing old whilst smashing up rocks.
Sewing mailbags till his fingers bled,
Behind a clanging door and lock.

Today, the psychologist tells us,
To excuse the poor misguided one.
He didn't really mean to do it,
He should be pitied, poor widow's son.

Give him a cell of his own,
With hi-fi and personal radio.
A chance to view communal TV.
A relaxing hour on the patio.

If today this is still termed Justice,
Then the scales are heavily tipped.,
In favour of those with gun and knife,
No wonder we are all tight-lipped!

*Len Hurle*

## OPEN AIR CAFÉ

A man sits at an Open Air Café
reading a newspaper
with nothing to say
An old lady appears
she holds out her hand
begging for money
in a foreign land

A girl sits at the Open Air Café
reading a magazine
with nothing to say
A stray dog appears
covered in sand
begging for food
in a foreign land

The man smiles at the girl in the Open Air Café
They both stop reading
and now have something to say
The waiter arrives cheerful and tanned
The beginning of love
in a foreign land

*Karen Anne Griffin*

## POETIC VISION

The poet by any other name
Demeaning or derided,
Misunderstood or acknowledged,
    Confided or indifferent,
    Friend or artist inspired
    Remains in name a poet.

So should remain true to self
Regardless of others,
Their comments and critique,
    Utterances oft' biased,
    Without true perception
    Of self-visions' crafted script.

*K Stanley Mallett*


## A VARIETY OF MUD

Plucked from Afrikaner dark,
By black pick excised.
Of Earth's entrails
The pallid prisoner diamond
Brightly taps a mood of greed,
Explodes rash light in flashy beads
To raid the poverty of sight
Of those whose eyes are mere lens,
Reducing vision to a precious stony reverence
And lust to own, of all mud's rich variety
This tight-tucked star pretence,
This pock of frozen spittle
Chattering of age and brilliance:
So cold, so hard, so little.

*Robert Moore*

## THE FOGHORN

I watched the fog approaching
Across the tranquil sea,
And soon the clammy vapour
Reached out engulfing me.

The chill air swirled about me,
Damp fingers at my throat,
As through the mist there echoed
The foghorn's mournful note.

Three blasts and then a silence
And then three blasts again
- The siren's melancholy,
Monotonous refrain.

It bellowed forth its warning
To sailors on the sea -
Beware the hidden danger,
beware calamity!

But even as it sounded
I heard a distant shout,
'Lord, help us in thy mercy!'
The awful cry went out.

Then all once more was quiet,
More quiet than before,
As I heard the sea awashing
Upon the sandy shore.

Again the foghorn sounded
its haunting, plaintive cry.
Was it, perhaps, bemoaning
The sailors who must die?

*Diane Hemp*

## REAL LIFE

Real life stands outside
A playground covered in autumn leaves
Children believing, bleeding
From broken knees
And the rain cries into puddles

Real life stands outside
A thousand phantoms
haunting schoolrooms
The teacher with the wooden leg
Striking fear into little hearts

Real life stands outside
As snow flakes fall
geography class disrupted
As the playground fills
With unmade snowballs

Real life stands outside
It can wait.

*P Gilson*


## TUTANKHAMUN

Tutankhamun
Tutankhamun,
taken from your shell.
Was this place your Heaven?
Or was it just your Hell?

Your vital organs removed,
your soul,
Untouched,
Unsoothed.

Was the face so beautiful
on your coffin lid?
Or was it so distorted,
a face that should be hid?

Bones in your casket, rotting away . . .
Fumes in your casket, endless decay . . .

Remember me!
Remember me!
The soul you have forgotten?
The soul you left for centuries?
The soul you left for rotting.

*J Morris*


## WHERE IS OUR RHYTHM

The ebb and flow that watchers keep
Ties us round a floating tree
We listen to the aiding wind
And perform to be once more set free.

Surrender to the hands of time
Knowingly fall on pumping palms
Feel the mood change that surrounds us
Expel and scatter the quiet calm.

Cruellest mind that wakes me often
Keep apart the truth and hope
Separate the honour from glory
Keep alive my wish to cope.

*Gil Matthews*

## THE GREAT ONE

What kind of power
Do you possess
Great Manitou
For I cannot see you
Nor touch you
I don't even know you
But you reach inside
And draw upon emotions
So deep
Effect on inner self
I cannot explain
Your aura draws me ever nearer
In the flesh I owe nothing
My spirit's of the inner world
Only know the truth
Great Chief
Of reactions unforetold
Secrets yet to be revealed
Veil themselves in your presence
I cannot tell you
What I feel
Your bonds of strength too tight
One day awareness will be unmasked
Till then
Great One
Till then . . .

*Aileen Kowal*

## BELOVED ISLE OF ENCHANTMENT

Beloved island where tranquillity and beauty reigns,
A land formed by God's creative hand.
A vivid dream, encaptured by romance,
A picture framed by times unfallen sands.

Oh fair isle whose luscious fields adorn her,
Whose crimson soil, burns upon her land.
Just as a story, filled with sweet enchantment,
Whose poetic words are caught within your mind.

Your flowing rivers entwine amid your forests,
Just like a pathway through the countless beauty of the night.
The silver moon rises high above your greenwood hills,
Like a mystic guardian of beauty and legend's plight.

Each fathom of your rolling sapphire ocean,
Reflects the golden aura, that surrounds your natural land.
Like a jewel enhanced with great emotion,
Whose power to re-create a dream is genuine and strong.

No artist's brush can paint your alluring beauty,
No flowing pen can describe your captive charm.
For whom of man can paint or write of heaven,
Of which my enchanting island is a part.

*Gillian Booker*

## FREEDOM

Behind iron bars
No open door
Kept from the world
Freedom no more.

Shut in the dark
No warmth or space
The world outside
A better place.

I had a dream
My life was mine
But there's a price to pay
For committing a crime.

So as you lay
Awake at night,
Think of your freedom
Hold it tight.

No mind to think
No eyes to see
If you pray tonight
Then pray for me.

*Nicola Cairns*


## THE SCENT OF MONEY

It wasn't that she put on airs,
Or made them feel so small.
her manners were impeccable,
but they knew she'd had it all.

Her dresses were so out of date,
The fabric was so fine.
Understatement was the theme,
It was all in the line.

'That fur coat must have cost a bomb'.
Said Marlene in despatch.
She'd had the mink for twenty years.
For winter there's no match.

Some said 'What is she doing here?'
Or 'She's unsuitable.
She hasn't ever been to school.
How does she know it all'.

She couldn't disguise her origins.
Or put her past away.
The scent of money retained its hold.
For which she had to pay.

*G Birmingham*


## WOMBLING FREE?
*(In memory of Rachel, R I P )*

Everyone's heard of the Wombles,
Living beneath the ground,
They make good use of the rubbish
And litter that's lying around.

They tidy up Wimbledon Common,
Or so the stories say;
Their innocent world has been shattered
With the girl that was murdered today.

*Sarah Phinn*

## THE TEAM

Work awaits
Four shire and a man
A team of love and strength
The plough so sharp and clean
Rings out as it cuts
'Walk on Captain, steady Boxer'
Gentle giants slowly tread
'Easy Prince, Easy Duke'
God's ground neatly folded slice on slice
The clink of flint on steel
The jangle of bridle and bit
All noises of the day now lost
Flat cap dries the sweating brow
Hobnails walk in silence
Gulls swoop and wail with mouths so wide
The cuckoo calls in infant light
Mist floats above the stubbled fields
As the hours go by
The pace never drops
Never too fast, never too slow
Man trusts horse, horse trusts man
They are the family of the countryside
They are as one.

*Basil Figura*

## TRIP TO PSYCHOSIS

The maniac hides his rotting face
As his loveless soul yearns for flesh.
An unholy sacrilege,
Blasphemy of the ultimate kind.
The urge to kill, to rape, to purge,
To murder peace of mind.

His anger and grief destroyed
His love and now his hope is lost.
A smile of Death
An abnormal knowledge of disconnection,
That killing grin, the violent sin,
Hates bloody face in reflection.

Blood holds no price but life itself
Is there to be rejected.
And victims in the cooling room
In their deaths give life to flies.
Certainly ironic, stinking, rancid, chronic,
As they lay eggs, eat, shit and die.

Vulgar are his dispositions.
Hatred fuelled his freezing fire.
And now reality fades.
Once more into the fuckin' world of pain.
Psychotic personality,  Schizophreniac reality
But none of his friends will believe he's insane!

No-one will ever understand.
No-one will ever understand.
No-one will ever stand!

*J C Hulls*

## EMPTY CAVERNS

Empty night that love
Has shrugged 'neath cotton, chilling sheets
Where lonely shadows creep
Set to spring
Surprise attacks of wondrous clarity
That bounce from every corner
Of this maze tormented mind.
At every twist and turn
Memories in warming bottles
Bubble and spill
To wet a crumpled pillow
That cannot share
Such unquenchable pain.
Delinquent voices searing through my head
Of what could and should and might have been,
When all I love rejected my caress
And this body shall no longer drink
From love's warm fountain.
Beyond this night
There is no sun-warmed day.
Endless, empty caverns
Where love has walked away.

*Kim Montia*


## TALL, DARK ...

Tall, dark and handsome, the fairy tale kind,
You know me by heart - read my mind.
You can guess what I'm thinking by a glance at my eyes,
brush off my sarcasm - but that won't die!

That sharp sense of humour, and cute sideways grin,
rolled up into one, how lucky I've been.
These feelings I've got - they're strange and so new,

Deep,

Strong,

True,

Perfection . . . that's you.

***Amanda Hall***


## BUXTON

I live in a village, a rural nook
Where beauty abounds wherever you look,
The trees all around are majestic and tall
Their boughs reaching out to embrace you all.

Horses graze in green fields all around
Anglers fish without making a sound,
You may row on the river at a leisurely pace
How lucky I am to live in this place.

We have a church, a school and some stables too
The village hall adjoins the park, there is always plenty to do,
Through the shaded leafy dell we love to walk
You will always find someone with whom to talk.

Not too built up that is good for a start
A special place to raise children and your lives to chart,
Some like a rat-race, noise and fumes all day
But slow down, look around you, give me Buxton any day!

***Sharon H Robinson***

# INFORMATION

We hope you have enjoyed reading this book - and that you will continue to enjoy it in the coming years.

If you like reading and writing poetry drop us a line, or give us a call, and we'll send you a free information pack.

Write to

Poetry Now Information
1-2 Wainman Road
Woodston
Peterborough
PE2 7BU